JUST MEDITATION

JUST MEDITATION

EVERYDAY MEDITATION FOR EVERYONE

NICHOLAS BUXTON

Magic Monastery Publishing
Quaker House
Durham
DH1 1XD
United Kingdom

First Published 2020

ISBN: 978-1-8381028-0-7
Epub ISBN: 978-1-8381028-1-4

Cover design Nicholas Buxton

For everyone who has been part of this journey

CONTENTS

Imagine a world in which everybody wears glasses. Only, these glasses do not enhance our vision, they impede it.

Some wear glasses with lenses so dark that all they can see is shadows, whilst others have lenses that are brightly coloured, yet no less distorting.

Some have glasses that are cracked and frosted, or so thickly encrusted with grime that they can hardly see anything at all. Others have glasses that are like mirrors, so that everywhere they look all they see is themselves.

And, because we have never known any different, we accept the world as it appears through our glasses, imagining that's the way it is.

But it isn't. And so, with vision impaired, we bump up against life, again and again, until the pain becomes normal.

But it's not. And in occasional moments of clarity, we can see that. But still we keep stumbling along, bumping into everything…

The solution would appear to be simple. Remove the glasses! Yet, somehow, that's the one thing we never think of.

This book is about how to do that.

INTRODUCTION

Saturday 12 October 2013. About a dozen people gathered in the upstairs room of the Recovery Centre, in what was once the old Coroner's Court, on the quayside by the Swing Bridge in Newcastle upon Tyne. We were there for a meditation workshop that I had volunteered to facilitate. The format was simple, accessible and inclusive. We sat in a circle. We introduced ourselves. I gave a short talk. There was some sharing and listening. And we meditated. There was no jargon; nobody was required to buy into any belief system. We just meditated. In silence.

In those days I was the vicar of a church in the city centre, with a particular remit for social responsibility. In due course, I met Ollie Batchelor, who was at that time operations director of a major regional homelessness charity, and we began a conversation about religion, spirituality, addiction and recovery. Together we decided to organise some sort of meditation workshop for a group of people we thought might be interested. Although it was only intended as a one-off, when everyone started asking when the next meeting was going to be, we decided to make it a regular monthly event. Over the next three years, the group continued to flourish and grow, requiring us to move to a larger venue. We never advertised—people just heard about the sessions by word of mouth—but we were often over-subscribed. Clearly there was something about what we were doing, and perhaps also the way we were doing it, that simply worked. I would maintain that this was because we were addressing an intrinsically spiritual need, and that such needs are a fundamental part of being human, though I accept that not everybody would necessarily see things in those terms.

Long before holding that first meditation workshop, I had for some years been thinking about how people might be able to satisfy their spiritual hunger in a society in which many conventional forms of spirituality, such as may be found in mainstream faith traditions, no longer seem to appeal to the majority of people. There are many and complex reasons for the apparent decline of religious adherence in western societies. But if it is true that human beings are spiritual creatures —just as we are also scientific, political and artistic creatures —then it follows that we have innate spiritual needs that remain in need of fulfilment, even in a supposedly secular society. This could explain the explosion of interest and activity in alternative spirituality, yoga, mindfulness, counselling and all things 'spiritual but not religious', which we now see filling the void left by the retreat of 'organised religion'. Another explanation might be that we are in the middle of a paradigm shift in the evolution of consciousness. I have to admit, I remain unpersuaded by the latter claim, widely held though it may be. It is far from clear that consciousness, in itself, and whatever it may be, is the sort of thing that actually 'evolves' at all. Nor is there any reason to think of evolution as a process with a purpose. Indeed, if we're using human behaviour as a measure of our 'evolutionary progress', then there is at least as much evidence to suggest the exact opposite.

That said, and regardless of how we might try to explain our current predicament, the question of how best to meet our spiritual needs still requires an answer. How can we engage with ancient wisdom traditions in ways that are relevant and accessible to people who can't or won't relate to the religious institutions that have historically provided a way in? Where can we encounter something a bit more nourishing than the type of consumer spirituality that so often seems like the spiritual equivalent of junk food? I now had a clear idea of what I thought might be a solution: an independent high street meditation centre. This would be a place wholly dedicated to the learning and practise of meditation, in a central urban location, that didn't require anyone to subscribe to any particular belief system, whether 'spiritual' or 'secular'.

Of course, there are already lots of places to learn and practise meditation. These include Buddhist groups, retreat centres, and even churches, which between them provide a wide variety of welcoming and accessible opportunities to meditate. But since such places are invariably part of some other—usually religious—organisation, at some point a belief system will be promoted in the hope that casual enquirers might become committed subscribers. This is entirely to be expected. But not everyone wants that. On top of this, there seems to be an assumption that to do it 'properly' you really need to go away on retreat somewhere. There are many excellent reasons for making time to go on retreat, but the simple truth of the matter is that not everybody has the opportunity. And in any case, isn't meditation all about being present? Why then does it always seem to be about being somewhere else?

My thinking was thus motivated by two principal imperatives. First, the need for an approach to meditation that was independent and inclusive. That is to say, ideologically neutral, neither belonging to nor promoting—or, for that matter, rejecting—any particular belief system, whether religious or other. And second, the need for it to be simple and accessible: on the high street and at the heart of everyday life. After a quick trawl of available internet domain names, the idea of Just Meditation was born.

PART I

WHAT IS MEDITATION

GETTING STARTED

Depending on how you look at it, meditation is either very complicated or very simple. On the one hand, there would appear to be a huge range of different phenomena variously described as 'meditation', from religious devotions to psychological exercises. On the other hand, meditation can be seen as something very straightforward: as easy as just sitting, just breathing, or even just *being*. The term can be applied to practices as varied as creative visualisations, guided meditations, chanting, repetition of prayers and mantras, thinking deeply about spiritual or philosophical ideas, mindfulness, relaxation techniques and concentration exercises, as well as physical disciplines such as yoga and tai chi. All these, and more, can be associated with the term 'meditation'. And yet, at the same time, although there seem to be so many different styles or techniques of meditation, in many cases they can be seen as having similar basic principles, common objects and related outcomes.

That said, at first glance, the sheer variety of traditions and teachings certainly seems bewildering, especially to anybody trying to learn about meditation for the first time. How should one choose between insight or mindfulness meditation? Which is the best out of mantra chanting or Tantric visualisations? What are we supposed to make of the competing claims of Christians and Buddhists, psychologists and new agers? Whose teachings can we trust from among the various popular 'brands' on offer? How will I know it's the real thing? And where can I go that's not going to be full of weirdos?

This uncertainty is likely to be compounded by the claims made for the benefits of meditation by advocates of particular teachings or traditions, which range from the fairly modest to the wildly extravagant. For some it is primarily a tool for reducing stress and aiding relaxation. For others it is about improving performance or acquiring spiritual insight or wisdom. And the various health benefits, both mental and physical, are almost too numerous to mention. If we are to believe the hype, meditation is the cure for all manner of ills from depression to heart disease. It is to be applied to anything and everything, from coping with stress to gaining a competitive edge in business, and it promises the fulfilment of our every desire, from better sex to the knowledge of God.

However, the real issue here is not that there are so many different techniques, but our tendency to think about meditation in terms of techniques and benefits in the first place. Meditation is not just a technique, which—if only it is practised correctly—will deliver certain specific outcomes. It is not a transaction but a discipline, in the sense of a skill or training. I didn't take up meditation in order to achieve a particular goal, choosing a technique according the results promised, but in order to learn something about being human – including the folly of wanting to find the 'best' meditation technique! Meditation is not just about all the benefits we may acquire as a result of following a certain set of exercises, but wholeness and healing, balance and perspective, and becoming a more fully integrated person. A preoccupation with techniques and results will inevitably keep our attention focussed on the idea of the self who will be the beneficiary of those outcomes, whereas the whole point of meditation is to take the focus *away* from the self. It is about dissolving and transcending the sense of self rather than feeding and reinforcing it. By stepping back from the fantasy world of our thoughts, we learn to see things as they are rather than as we think they should or shouldn't be. Ultimately, we learn to break free from the prison of the ego.

Freedom, albeit variously conceived, is the common goal of a great number of different meditation disciplines. Freedom from stress and anxiety, from fear and insecurity. Freedom from our habitual tendency to make a mess of things. Freedom from our slavery to misplaced desires. Freedom from the fantasies and delusions that control us. If we must look at meditation in terms of outcomes, let's look at the big picture. Forget those long, detailed lists of all the supposed benefits of meditation; look for the one thing that will make a real difference. Once we start seeing things like this, we may also notice that by and large most meditation practices not only have the same goal but also work in a similar way. Most forms of meditation generally involve occupying the attention somehow— such as by focussing on a single object of experience—in order to cultivate certain states of mind, such as awareness, insight or serenity. These two factors, namely a conscious intention to encourage, or even just allow, the mind to settle and become calm, whilst at the same time enabling our awareness to expand and deepen by simply letting thoughts come and go without getting caught up in them, are the basic ingredients of the Just Meditation approach.

By the simple act of deliberately anchoring our attention to one thing, whilst trying to avoid being distracted by everything else, we are able to cultivate at least some degree of mental tranquillity. We do this not just for its own sake, though there is undoubtedly benefit in that, but in order to develop insight into the way things are and to grow in awareness as a result. By allowing the mind to become settled and calm, we also enable clarity and insight to arise. By seeing things more clearly, especially our own thoughts, feelings and behaviour, we learn to live life more skilfully, manage difficult emotions and make better decisions. By cultivating greater self-awareness we become less self-centred and more present, not only to our own experience but also to the experience of others. The process of going into the self paradoxically leads us out of the self. To be self-aware is necessarily to be aware of the common experience of being human that we all share. As a consequence, meditation releases our innate capacity for compassion and connection. This is why meditation is not just a lot of self-indulgent navel-gazing. Quite the opposite in fact. It has an unavoidably ethical dimension. As our practice changes our behaviour, so it will naturally affect those around us as well. If it doesn't, one might well be forgiven for wondering what it's for. Meditation is about cultivating calmness and clarity, compassion and connection. More than simply a handy technique to help us relax, it is in truth nothing less than the solution to the problem of the human condition.

COMMON (MIS)UNDERSTANDINGS

Meditation is more widely practised today than ever before. Having once been seen as a 'fringe' activity, together with related disciplines such as yoga and mindfulness, it is now very much part of mainstream western culture. And yet, a number of common misconceptions remain prevalent, resulting in a good deal of confusion about exactly what it is, how you do it, and why it might be a good thing to do in the first place. Among the most enduring of those misconceptions are the notions that meditation is about emptying the mind, thinking of nothing, or going into a trance. Even if we disregard those traditions of meditation that explicitly *do* involve actively thinking about something, as well as guided meditations and visualisations, this could still hardly be further from the truth. The notion that one can simply empty one's mind, or think of nothing, is rapidly dispelled as soon as one tries to do it.

Whilst it is certainly true that meditation very often entails somehow focussing the attention on one thing, that doesn't mean all other mental activity simply stops. If only it were that easy! The mind continues to think, to process mental

data, because that is what the mind is. And it cannot be otherwise. For the same reason it is also quite impossible to think
of nothing, for that would either require another thought, or it
would imply the mind's non-existence – both of which would
be utterly contradictory. What meditation *does* often involve is
an intention to keep the attention occupied by, or focussed on,
a single object in order to settle and calm the mind. At the
same time, we let thoughts come and go without getting
personally involved in them, thus allowing clarity to emerge
from the stillness. The distinction between this and not
thinking may be a subtle one, but it is all-important. Thoughts
continue to come and go, whether we want them to or not—
and it could hardly be otherwise—but we do not have to get
caught up in the story, we do not have to *become* our thoughts.

STEREOTYPES

Meditation has undoubtedly become more mainstream, and
this is surely a positive development. It is no longer the exclusive preserve of Buddhist monks, Christian contemplatives
and Hindu yogis; nor is it confined to the sub-cultures of new
age and alternative spirituality. The recent explosion in popularity of mindfulness, and its widespread acceptance across
many different sectors—from the medical establishment to
the military—has raised the profile of meditation and
extended its appeal to people who might not otherwise have
considered it to be of interest to them. In spite of all of that,
however, meditation still suffers from a serious image problem. In the popular imagination, it continues to be associated
with the so called 'hippy culture' of the 1960s and 70s, and all
the pejorative connotations this is sometimes meant to imply.
Admittedly, this particular cliché has become less prevalent in
recent years, as the popularisation of mindfulness has enabled
meditation to migrate from counter culture to consumer

culture. Yet the representation of meditation in the media remains stubbornly unregenerate. Beaches, lakes and mountain ranges provide the typical backdrop for attractive models —usually female, often blonde—to pose in contrived and sometimes rather uncomfortable looking postures, whilst pretending to meditate.

This ubiquitous and somewhat predictable stereotype is unhelpful in two significant ways. First, it suggests that meditation is the preserve of a middle-class elite: young, good looking and blessed with the financial wherewithal to enjoy holidays in exotic locations. It makes meditation the equivalent of a spa treatment: a pleasurable reward, like cocktails by the pool, for those who have left the difficulties of life behind them, or just because they deserve the gift of 'self care' or 'me time'. Second, it implies that meditation is something that you do somewhere else, meaning that it is therefore not part of normal everyday life. We can see further evidence of this attitude in the trend for contemporary meditation spaces to be designed in such a way that they completely cut out any external distractions with windowless, sound-proofed rooms, mood lighting, and a range of guided meditations on headphones. It's not hard to understand why meditation tends to be marketed like this, but the irony is that it is then perceived as something that is entirely *separate* from the reality of the here and now, rather than the discipline of engaging more fully with it. This is meditation as a tool for self-improvement, a spiritual commodity re-branded as yet another aspirational lifestyle accessory, or reduced to little more than a motivational technique to increase productivity or achieve personal goals.

Meditation is not about escaping from 'the world', or fulfilling a consumerist agenda for 'self-development', but living life more skilfully and with greater integrity. It is not just a stress-busting technique for busy executives, but an opportunity to take a step back from ourselves in order to see things as they really are, rather than as we think we would like them to be. Meditation is not merely a therapeutic intervention to address the symptoms of a problem, while leaving the causes untouched, but a means for transforming the whole of life. It is not about self-indulgence, personal fulfilment or improving efficiency but self-awareness, balance, perspective, wholeness and healing. Meditation is neither exotic nor exclusive: it is for anyone and everyone, and it belongs firmly at the heart of everyday life.

DEFINITIONS

Meditation is a word that today is most often used to refer to various disciplines of mental and spiritual cultivation frequently, though not exclusively, derived from Yoga and Buddhism. To be more specific, it is the English word generally used to translate the terminology relating to these practices from Sanskrit and other Asian languages. As teachings derived from Eastern spiritual traditions became increasingly popular in western societies during the second half of the twentieth century, so it is primarily in connection with these traditions, and subsequent developments from them, that the word is typically used today.

But, of course, 'meditation' is also an English word in its own right that was in everyday use long before most people in the west were even aware of the Asian spiritual traditions with which the word is now most commonly associated. In ordinary English usage 'meditation' simply means 'to think deeply' about something, for example mulling over a passage of scripture or a knotty metaphysical problem. This is how the term has historically been understood in the context of Christian spirituality and the western cultural and philosophical tradition. This is also why we use the word to describe any kind of thoughtful reflection on a particular theme. A film or a book, for example, could be described as a meditation on time, or love, or whatever.

The actual word 'meditation' comes from the Latin *meditatio*, which refers to the act of thinking or pondering. It is sometimes suggested that the Latin verb *meditari*, to think or reflect upon, is also related to the words *mederi*, to heal, and *metiri*, to measure, both of which provide us with fruitful ways of thinking about meditation. The former, *mederi*, which gives us words like medical and medicine, reinforces the familiar notion of meditation as a prescription for spiritual health and wellbeing. It is no coincidence that so many of the world's great spiritual teachers are thought of as healers. For example, the Buddha was described metaphorically as a physician and Jesus was famous for his healing miracles. The latter, *metiri*, from which we get words for measurement, such as meter and metric, denotes the idea of meditation as something to do with putting things into perspective and seeing them as they really are. Thus, thinking about meditation in terms of healing implies the sense of restoring balance and wholeness in our lives, whilst the notion of measuring conveys the idea of putting things into perspective. It also reminds us of how we talk about getting the measure of something in the sense of coming to an understanding of it. Indeed, it is interesting to note the extent to which, in one way or another, measuring things is so central to many aspects of human endeavour. In ordinary everyday life we are constantly asking how much, how long, how far or how many? So much of what we do involves quantifying—in other words, measuring—the relationship between things. This is no less true of our practise of meditation, which has as one of its primary objectives the cultivation of greater harmony in our relationship to the world in which we find ourselves, and the other people with whom we share it.

Another word we may sometimes encounter in this context is contemplation. Just to confuse things, this is the term sometimes used in the western tradition to denote the sort of practices that most closely correspond to the eastern disciplines we commonly refer to as 'meditation'. To contemplate, from the Latin *contemplatio*, has meanings that include to observe, look at, or pay attention to something. This seems to fit rather well with the kind of meditation practices that involve focussing the attention on a particular object, or simply being aware of the content of consciousness. Indeed it could be argued that in many ways it is a more appropriate word to use for such practices than the word meditation itself, which as we have seen is really to do with *thinking* about something: the exact opposite of what we're trying to do when we meditate! That said, meditation is the word commonly used, so that's what we'll stick with.

THE MINDFULNESS MOVEMENT

There is, of course, another word, namely mindfulness, that is frequently associated with meditation. But are they the same? Are they different? And if so, how and in what way? One thing's for sure: mindfulness has come a long way from its origins as a type of Buddhist meditation. Nowadays it is generally seen as something that is completely different to meditation – and nothing to do with Buddhism either. And yet, whilst it is certainly true that 'mindfulness' and 'meditation' are words that can be, and frequently are, used in different ways, I would suggest there is also a good deal of overlap between them as well. After all, one of the principal aims of meditation is to cultivate mindfulness, and one of the principal means of cultivating mindfulness is meditation. Therefore, if you go to a mindfulness class the chances are that you will, amongst other things, learn something about meditation; and if you go to a meditation class the chances are that you will, amongst other things, learn how to be more mindful.

And yet, the fact remains that in the popular understanding mindfulness and meditation are clearly viewed by many people as being entirely distinct. This may be because, as we have seen, the word meditation can be used in a great variety of different ways, not all of which would necessarily involve the cultivation of mindfulness. And mindfulness can be cultivated in all sorts of ways, not all of which necessarily involve formal meditation practice. In addition, it sometimes seems that mindfulness is perceived as being somehow more secular, more accessible, perhaps easier: something for the non-specialist. No doubt this is in part a result of the explosion in the popularity and inevitable commodification of mindfulness, which has resulted in it being extended to an ever-wider range of applications, some of them—some might think—slightly superficial. Meditation, by comparison, seems sometimes to be perceived as being more difficult, requiring more effort or commitment, something for specialists, and something that might also be identified as a religious or spiritual practice.

These distinctions are not entirely without foundation, though I'm not sure they are particularly helpful either. I prefer to see mindfulness as an outcome of meditation, and meditation as the practice of mindfulness. In order to unpack this a bit more it may help to identify two principal ways in which the word mindfulness tends to be used. On the one hand, it describes an attitude of being present, attentive and aware, as a state of mind or way of being in the world. On the other, it denotes various practices, whether explicitly Buddhist or supposedly secular, including but not limited to meditation, aimed at cultivating that attitude, state of mind or way of being in the world.

Long before the advent of Mindfulness Based Stress Reduction programmes, mindfulness colouring books, mindful dieting, mindful dating and the ubiquity of mindfulness programmes in education, healthcare and the workplace, mindfulness was just an ordinary English word, generally used to denote being attentive, conscious or aware of something. It has existed in the English language since late medieval times as a word for being recollected; literally, 'of good memory'. Hence, in everyday speech, we might use the word when talking about bearing something in mind or being careful – which, of course, implies paying attention to whatever it might be. We also frequently use the term to refer to being aware of others, as in being mindful of someone's feelings, for example. In relation to contemporary mindfulness practice, it retains all of those meanings, denoting both the state of being present to and fully engaged with reality as it is, as well as the various techniques designed to cultivate an attitude of attentive awareness, or being in the now. And, of course, it is also the word that was chosen to translate the terminology of the Buddhist meditation teachings from which those contemporary mindfulness techniques have been derived.

Sometimes it can be helpful to explore the meaning of a term by considering its opposite. In this case, the opposite of being mindful would include being mindless, such as when we do things without really thinking about what we are doing. How much time do we spend distractedly swiping through social media posts on our mobile devices? How much do we miss as we go through life with our head down, looking at a screen? Another example of the opposite of mindfulness would be absent mindedness, such as when we are so preoccupied by our own thoughts that we do not notice what is going on around us, or we forget what we're doing because we are daydreaming or not paying attention. How many times have we walked past someone we know without realising it? Or suddenly been caught out when we're not really listening to what someone is saying? Finally, there is the opposite of mindfulness in the sense of being in a state of oblivion. As well as the obvious fact that we can hardly be mindful if we are inebriated, or unconscious, this also reminds us that meditation is not about not thinking, or emptying the mind, but being more fully aware and present to reality as it actually is. The fact is that much of the time we are quite oblivious to what is going on: we are literally not present. And if we are going through life on autopilot, we are not really living at all.

By contrast, we can be more mindful in all sorts of ordinary everyday ways, such as by deliberately paying more attention to our surroundings, our routine daily tasks, and other people. Learning to be more mindful, in the ordinary sense of the word, is the purpose of the formal practice of mindfulness meditation. In other words, the point of meditation is to cultivate the state of mindfulness, of being more aware, more present—to oneself and the world around us—and remembering to apply that awareness in everyday life.

CONTEMPORARY SECULAR MINDFULNESS

The word 'mindfulness' is most commonly used today to refer to a particular programme of meditation exercises and associated wellbeing practices. Originally developed as a therapeutic intervention for the relief of pain, stress and related medical conditions, it has also been applied as a self-help technique to improve performance and efficiency in a wide variety of unrelated contexts. Indeed, such is the popularity of mindfulness that it has been touted as the panacea for all things – from stress and anxiety to making better business decisions. It is, for the most part, presented in strictly secular and psychological terms, and has been adopted—with mixed results—within healthcare, education, commerce and even the military. It is, apparently, good for everything from weight loss to the corporate bottom line.

Mindfulness, in this context, is typically defined in terms of cultivating non-judgmental awareness, in the present moment, by paying deliberate attention to our immediate experience, as it is, with open-minded curiosity and acceptance of that experience for what it is. Although derived from traditional Buddhist meditation teachings, contemporary secular mindfulness has largely discarded any explicit reference to the Buddhist doctrines that originally provided mindfulness meditation with its *raison d'être*. Whether fundamentally Buddhist assumptions remain implicit within secular mindfulness teachings is open to debate, however. Depending on the audience, leading figures in the mindfulness movement sometimes make a point of describing secular mindfulness as Buddhism in disguise, whilst at other times going to great lengths to play down any hint of Buddhist influence, appealing instead to the authority of 'science'. Indeed, some mindfulness teachers seem so keen to disassociate themselves from Buddhism that they will blatantly deny that mindfulness has any connection with Buddhism whatsoever. It is presented simply as a product of modern psychology: a tool to reduce stress, ease pain, improve sleep, promote wellbeing and enhance productivity. Yet, it is perfectly clear—and, given the history of the development of contemporary secular mindfulness, not at all surprising—that concepts derived from Buddhist teachings permeate even the most dogmatically secular mindfulness discourses.

Aspects of the contemporary mindfulness phenomenon have predictably drawn a certain amount of criticism, with some Buddhists, in particular, feeling that their tradition has been hijacked for questionable purposes. Many of these criticisms claim that the absence of a philosophical or ethical context in the application of mindfulness devalues the practice, or even renders it meaningless, because the part played by our intentions is thereby ignored. After all, good surgeons need a high degree of mindfulness in order to do their job, but that doesn't necessarily make them enlightened. In Buddhism, by contrast, mindfulness meditation is set within a wider context that includes a moral imperative. Intention is what determines whether any given action is good or bad, wholesome or unwholesome, conducive to enlightenment or not. One can therefore practice mindfulness for the 'right' reasons and one can practice it for the 'wrong' reasons, and we should expect the outcome to vary accordingly. In a Buddhist worldview all things are interconnected, and the practice of meditation is not just a personal self-help technique but a spiritual discipline intended to transform our understanding of the meaning and purpose of human existence.

Others have been critical of the excessive commodification of mindfulness—it is routinely used as a marketing gimmick for a wide range of unrelated products and services—as well as numerous applications of mindfulness that seem at best rather trivial or self-indulgent. Sometimes characterised as 'McMindfulness', this is mindfulness as a quick fix to help us feel good about ourselves rather than a long-term programme of radical self-transformation that also impacts the world around us. Some have identified an even more sinister aspect of the contemporary secular mindfulness movement that ironically suggests a presumably unintentional collusion with the unhealthy conditions it purports to address. The emphasis on accepting the reality of the present moment, without judging it good or bad, could induce a degree of compliance with situations that actually do need challenging, or encourage the endorsement of delusion rather than the resolve to expose it. For example, the promotion of mindfulness in the workplace to alleviate stress could be viewed as a cynical attempt to pacify the workforce and increase productivity without actually doing anything to address the systemic causes of stress, such as poor working conditions, low pay or lack of job security. Placing the burden of responsibility on the individual shifts it away from the toxic corporate culture that is liable for the situation in the first place. Cloaked with the pseudo-religious authority of 'science', mindfulness becomes a means of maintaining the status quo and reinforcing the hegemony of consumer capitalism, rather than the key to genuine liberation.

Instead of talking about learning to accept things as they are, I prefer to talk about learning to *see* things as they are. And that can be very different. Rather than blindly accepting everything, seeing what's what gives us the ability to decide how best to respond or relate to whatever it might be. Learning to see things as they are implies a willingness to accept that things are, in fact, as they are, rather than how we think they should or shouldn't be, but it doesn't mean they can't be challenged. Sometimes we do indeed need to learn to accept things we might not want to accept. But there may be other circumstances where we have, perhaps over time, come to accept things which we shouldn't accept and ought to change. Seeing things more clearly, gaining a little objectivity and critical perspective, and learning to put our ego to one side, gives us the necessary discernment that enables us to choose how to act, rather than always and only blindly reacting.

To be fair, whilst there are those who see contemporary secular mindfulness in terms of the exploitation of selected elements of Buddhist teaching and practice, divorced from the wider context within which those practices obtain their meaning and purpose, others see the mindfulness phenomenon as a legitimate development in the continuing evolution of the Buddha dharma in the West. Both views no doubt make valid points. Whichever way one looks at it, however, the popularity of contemporary secular mindfulness has done much to raise the profile of meditation and related practices, encouraging many who might not otherwise have engaged with such teachings to learn something of benefit to them. And that is surely a good thing. Clearly, a growing number of people have found mindfulness and meditation to be of great value in relation to a wide range of conditions, thereby contributing to their general wellbeing, health and happiness. Some may even have been encouraged to take things further, perhaps by exploring a spiritual tradition more deeply. And yet the application of mindfulness to ever more novel objectives—including weight loss, commercial success or sexual fulfilment—does seem to be in tension with the intended purposes of mindfulness meditation practice within the context from which it originally came, so it is to this that we now turn.

MINDFULNESS IN BUDDHISM

Contemporary secular mindfulness is usually described in terms of non-judgmental awareness, or being present to the content of consciousness, as it is in itself, without adding a layer of commentary or evaluation. And one can easily see how this formula has been derived from Buddhist meditation teachings. Both Buddhism and contemporary secular mindfulness emphasise the cultivation of present moment awareness, and paying attention to the reality of experience, without analysis or interpretation. However, that may be as far as the similarity goes.

In Buddhism the Sanskrit word *sati*, usually translated as 'mindfulness', is—like the English word mindfulness—a term for memory. To remember something is to bring it to mind, make it present to consciousness. In the context of Buddhist meditation teachings, mindfulness suggests the notion of being present, or recollected, to the reality of the way things are, which—by extension—also means being recollected to the truths articulated in Buddhist teachings. And this is where we start to see some of the principal differences emerge between mindfulness in Buddhism and mindfulness in a secular context, whether that be in healthcare, the workplace or the pursuit of personal development. Buddhist teachings on mindfulness cannot be separated from the wider context of Buddhist doctrine, which gives those teachings their meaning and purpose, without compromising their integrity. The emphasis and degree might vary between different schools and traditions but, on the whole, mindfulness in Buddhism is not just about cultivating a state of bare attention alone and for its own sake. Rather, it is about cultivating attention, awareness and clarity of mind in order to gain insight into the true nature of things—according to the principal tenets of Buddhism—that is, the impermanence, unsatisfactoriness and lack of essential being that characterise the whole of existence.

It is sometimes said that the Buddha taught only two things: suffering and the cessation of suffering. This isn't quite true, as it happens, though these are certainly core themes. He clearly taught a great many other things as well, which is why the collected teachings of the Buddha take up nearly two metres of shelf space. The point being that mindfulness in Buddhism is part of a highly sophisticated worldview, and it has a very specific role within it: namely, to purify the mind in order to see things more clearly and, ultimately, to resolve the problem of the human condition. In Buddhist terms this means seeing the transient, empty, contingent and provisional nature of all things, including—or, in fact, especially—our own selves. Meditation, in Buddhism, is rather more than a coping mechanism for stress. It is about learning to see things the way they really are—in particular, the constructs of the self that keep us bound to our suffering—in order to attain liberation from the beginningless, endless cycle of karma and rebirth. Insight arises from the practise of being present to reality as it is, seeing things clearly and without attachment, which is to say, without allowing notions of selfhood, of I, me and mine, to arise. Furthermore, mindfulness in Buddhism is inextricably linked to the ethical dimension of Buddhist teachings: it is an essential component of the good life. If one's meditation practice does not lead to the development of wisdom and compassion, and thus contribute to making the individual a better person and the world a better place, then it is not 'right' mindfulness.

In other words, the fundamental purpose of mindfulness meditation in Buddhism is bound up with the religious goals of the Buddhist worldview, which we might summarise as learning to see through the illusions of the self in order to obtain release from the existential suffering inherent in worldly existence. To extract it from that context, and deploy it as a standalone therapeutic technique to address an altogether different set of issues and circumstances, inevitably raises a number of questions. Indeed, one cannot help but notice a certain discrepancy between the world transcending spiritual objectives of Buddhist meditation practice, and the rather more world affirming aspirations sometimes articulated within the contemporary secular mindfulness movement, where the emphasis seems to be not so much on enlightenment as enjoyment. Far from being a method of gaining release from the prison of the ego, contemporary secular mindfulness seems to be focussed on increasing one's ability to enjoy the pleasures of life, by means of mindful sex and enhanced business acumen. There is a certain irony in the fact that practices developed by and for monks vowed to poverty and celibacy, living under obedience to the strict rule of a monastic order and seeking to renounce all sensual desire, are now being marketed as the means of attaining financial success and physical gratification. And this really brings us to the crux of the matter. Mindfulness in Buddhism is not simply a matter of practising present moment awareness for its own sake, but learning to do so without giving rise to attachment, or the tendency to identify with, and define the self in terms of, all the various phenomena of our transitory experience, both physical and mental.

Recall the definition of mindfulness as non-judgmental awareness of the experience of the present moment, or paying attention on purpose and without analysis or evaluation. The notion of being aware, being present, is clear and easy enough to grasp, even if not always so easy to sustain. But exactly what is meant by the particular *kind* of awareness we are to cultivate—namely non-judgemental awareness—is perhaps slightly less clear. To say that mindfulness is about being aware of the content of consciousness without attributing any kind of value judgement, without categorising that experience in positive or negative terms, without getting involved in commentary and analysis, but just accepting it as it is, for what it is, is all well and good. But the point is that according to Buddhist teaching, the process of attributing value judgements to the various phenomena of experience— which we automatically do all the time—gives rise to a sense of identification with those phenomena as being I, me and mine. And it is this sense of self, the notion of the subject and 'owner' of our experience, that is the fundamental problem. In other words, it's not just about not engaging in commentary and evaluation, but gaining insight into the nature of the one who judges, the evaluator, and seeing that this too is another construct, another thought process that arises and ceases, like all other thoughts, as the result of a series of causes and conditions. Mindfulness is not just about non-judgmental awareness, as something rather passive and disengaged, but cultivating the clarity of mind that enables us to see the constructs of the self that make those judgements and evaluations in the first place. It is not just about cultivating 'bare attention' but a 'right view' of things, specifically a right view of the constructed self: the notion of I, me and mine in relation to the otherwise impersonal phenomena of experience.

The practice of mindfulness meditation in Buddhism involves rather more than simply being aware of the present moment. It is the means by which we learn to see and understand attachment, or the process by which the notion of the sense of self comes into being in the first place. The importance of grasping this point cannot be overemphasised, and we will return to it again in subsequent chapters. For now, let's just say that attachment, in this context, does not simply refer to the sentimental feelings we may have in relation to our favourite possessions. It is nothing less than the process by which we construct our sense of self by identifying with things that are not, in fact, who and what we really are. This includes the body and other material objects, as well as memories, thoughts, feelings, opinions, beliefs, achievements, hopes, fears, ambitions, relationships and so on. When we talk about attachment, we are talking about all the things that make me the 'me' that I am, including my education, family history, life experience, social conditioning, and personal dispositions; in other words, all the phenomena of experience that we designate as I, me, or mine.

This is where we see the greatest divergence between contemporary secular mindfulness and mindfulness in traditional Buddhist teachings. The latter emphasises renunciation and detachment in order to attain *nirvana*, the cessation of the fires of greed, hatred and delusion that perpetuate attachment and give rise to the suffering that is the inevitable consequence of our illusions of selfhood. The former, by contrast, can sometimes seem as if it is all about self-fulfilment and enhancing our enjoyment of life by paying more attention to our everyday sensory experiences. Not that there is anything wrong with enjoying the good things in life. It's just that making this our primary aim would be considered, in

Buddhist terms at least, a rather short-term goal that will inevitably, moreover, end in disappointment. Mindfulness in Buddhism is practised in order to gain insight into the way things are and, ultimately, to realise enlightenment. The application of mindfulness as a universal approach to the achievement of goals as varied as weight loss, parenting skills, sexual pleasure and business strategy, produces a strange hybrid that can perhaps best be understood as the assimilation of Buddhist meditation practices to the modern western religion of consumerism.

JUST MEDITATION

I was probably about fourteen years old when I first became aware of something called 'meditation'. I had no idea, really, what it was—never mind how to do it—but I can distinctly remember being under the impression that it had something to do with not thinking, or making the mind go blank, or concentrating on some featureless object, like a sheet of plain white paper. Why anyone would actually *want* to do this in the first place was not at all clear to me at the time, yet there must have been something about the idea of it that made me curious. Not long after that I found myself reading books about Buddhism, which, of course, further stimulated my growing interest in meditation—not to mention the appealling idea of reaching *nirvana*—though it would be some years before I finally got around to learning how to do it.

And so, inspired by some sort of hopelessly naïve quest to attain enlightenment, or at least to answer the 'big questions', I embarked upon the study of meditation and related disciplines, including yoga and, later still, Christian mysticism. Therefore, my interest in meditation began with, and has subsequently been sustained by, engagement with some of the world's great spiritual and religious traditions. Until relatively recently, this was probably more or less the route by which most people got into meditation. That should hardly come as any surprise. Although commonly associated with Buddhism, meditation also plays a central role in many schools of yoga, originating from Hindu traditions, as well as being analogous to contemplative prayer in Christianity, not to mention related practices in Judaism, Islam and other religions. Nowadays, however, most people are more likely to encounter meditation, or mindfulness, in a secular context, such as healthcare, education or the workplace, where it is usually presented as a coping mechanism or life skill: a therapeutic intervention rather than a spiritual discipline. As a result, many contemporary practitioners tend to play down the religious origins and spiritual dimensions of their practice, preferring to see what they do as a purely psychological technique to enhance wellbeing. There is nothing intrinsically wrong with this approach, and it arguably makes meditation more inclusive and accessible, but it does also risk shutting the door on what could turn out to be some very worthwhile avenues of enquiry. Regardless of whether our interest and involvement in meditation is grounded in a secular context, it nevertheless remains a fact that all the disciplines and techniques we generally associate with the word 'meditation'—including contemporary secular mindfulness—are derived, directly or indirectly, from the world's religious traditions. Moreover, this is no coincidence.

Whatever else a religion may be—and every religion is a great many things—it is, at least in part, a response to the fundamental and universal predicament of being human. The fact that, for whatever reason, human beings are endowed with minds, and not merely brains, gives us the ability to reflect on our experience, including the ultimately mysterious, irreducible and inexplicable fact of conscious existence itself. This capacity for self-awareness, unique—so we believe—to human beings, gives rise to what we might call the problem of the human condition: the instinctive knowledge of the all-pervasive unsatisfactoriness of life that is a direct consequence of the inevitable finitude of everything that is. Death is the common destiny of all living creatures, but the fact that as human beings we *know* this, and can engage in abstract speculation about it, would appear to be our particular blessing and curse. Although we are aware that we must one day die, we are, at the same time, paradoxically unable to conceive of our own non-existence. Just as the mind cannot not think, so being cannot comprehend non-being, which is why we have developed all the various beliefs we have about what happens when we die. The attempt to answer this most tantalising and yet impossible of riddles lies at the very root of what we might call the religious instinct. And, not surprisingly, we see the same impulse in newer forms of metaphysical speculation, such as may be articulated by the fantasies of science fiction. The revolt against mortality is what gives rise to the whole of human culture, all our arts and sciences, all our instincts and motivations, both collectively and individually. It is the driving force of life itself.

At the core of our being, therefore, lies a fundamental contradiction: the knowledge that ultimately we will not, and therefore in some sense do not, ultimately, exist. The various spiritual exercises we associate with the term 'meditation' can be seen as disciplines of personal transformation that people, in all times and places, have developed in response to questions of ultimate meaning and value. Contemplation on the mystery of being is the fundamental spiritual enterprise. Who are we? Why are we here? What are we meant to do about it? These are the unanswerable questions that lie at the heart of the world's religious traditions. Meditation and related spiritual exercises are the disciplines that enable us to grapple with those questions – though it can sometimes seem as if many religious people are so preoccupied with concerns about how to be religious that they barely even engage with these quintessentially religious questions at all!

For most of human history meditation has been seen as a specialised spiritual discipline for the religious professional. Now, however, teachings that were once the preserve of cloistered monks have become widely disseminated—in some cases altered beyond recognition—and applied to what we might call everyday use. Today, meditation can be approached from any number of different perspectives. For one person, it might be a tool they use to help them cope with stress. For another, it might be a spiritual discipline, whether within the context of a faith tradition or not. The Just Meditation approach seeks to be inclusive of these diverse perspectives—and all points in between—by neither promoting nor rejecting any particular spirituality, belief system or worldview. Just Meditation is completely independent, not being part of any other organisation, school or tradition. Nobody is required to 'buy into' the metaphysical assumptions of a religious or philosophical ideology. You can be a Christian, you can be an atheist. You can be Buddhist, Pagan, Sikh or Sufi. You can be nothing or anything—and still benefit from the practice—with no strings attached.

At the same time, whilst we don't *have* to make reference to the teaching of any particular spiritual tradition, and we certainly don't require assent to any religious beliefs, we can still acknowledge that there may be something of interest in those traditions, which could deepen our understanding and merit further exploration. Thus, whilst the Just Meditation approach is ideologically neutral, it is not dogmatically or reductively secularist. It does not try to deny that contemporary secular mindfulness is based on Buddhist teachings, for example. Rather, it freely acknowledges the significance of various wisdom traditions, and encourages further investigation as and when it might be relevant or informative to pursue such enquiries.

If the first principle is about an approach to meditation that is independent and inclusive, the second is about keeping it simple and making it accessible. Just Meditation is just what it says it is: a simple, no frills, meditation practice, involving focussing the attention on a single object, such as the breath or a mantra, whilst at the same time letting other thoughts come and go without getting involved in the story. It is a method that is suitable for absolute beginners, so simple that it can be taught in just a few minutes, and requiring no prior knowledge or beliefs. At the same time it is a practice that will last a lifetime or more, because it has a depth that is inexhaustible. In other words, the basic practice is the advanced practice. There are no higher teachings for the initiated. The technique is the same on day one as it is twenty years later. Sit quietly. Observe the breath. Repeat a mantra if that's helpful. Let the thoughts come and go, without getting caught up in them. That's it. The only variable is how far you take it, which is not about going somewhere else but going deeper into where you already are. So it's called 'Just Meditation' because that's what it is: neither exotic nor exclusive, but ordinary, accessible and available to all. It might not be the only meditation technique out there, but it's the only one you'll need.

If meditation is truly universal, then there is no need to complicate it with a lot of technical vocabulary or esoteric paraphernalia. If it is not something that pretty much anyone can do, whatever their circumstances, then what's the point of it? Meditation should not be seen as something that is only for special times and special places. It is not something that only happens somewhere else. And it is not something that is only for certain types of people. That's why we talk about Just Meditation as everyday meditation for everyone. It is everyday meditation in terms of the simple, straightforward way in which it is taught and practised, as well as in the sense that it should be seen as part of ordinary everyday life, and finally because it is something to be done literally every day.

ATTENTION AND AWARENESS

In spite of what may appear to be a great profusion of different types of meditation, most practices can be seen as having a relatively small number of common aims, many of which can be grouped under categories such as calmness and equanimity or clarity and insight. These correspond to the terms in which we defined meditation earlier: as being to do with wholeness and healing on the one hand, and balance and perspective on the other. Consequently, there are those practices that tend to emphasise concentration or focussing the attention on a single object of awareness, such as the breath, repetition of a mantra, or a visual image. The purpose of this is to train the mind to be steady, free from disturbance and distraction, in order to achieve single-pointed awareness and equanimity. Then, there are those practices that promote simply being aware of the experience of the present moment, without necessarily 'doing' anything at all. The aim here is not concentration, so much as just letting thoughts and experiences come and go without evaluation or interpretation, without getting involved in them, in order to allow the mind to become naturally tranquil and clear.

In some approaches to meditation it can seem as if one of these two aspects is prioritised over the other, such that one meditation technique may stress the development of concentration, whilst another may emphasise the cultivation of awareness; one may be aimed at calming the mind, another may be about clarity of mind. The Just Meditation approach, by contrast, seeks to combine rather than distinguish these two principles. Focussing the attention on a single object and dispassionately observing the content of consciousness are not to be seen as two separate techniques, but two aspects of the single practice of awareness. Both are necessary. Indeed, like two sides of a coin, you cannot have one without the other. The mind needs to be calm in order to see things clearly; the mind needs to be clear in order to experience calmness. It is not enough simply to practise intense concentration exercises if nothing is learnt about how the mind works because one is too busy forcing it to concentrate. This may be a good way to develop willpower, but it represents a rather limited approach to meditation. A certain amount of concentration is necessary, but a determined effort to concentrate is likely to become another mental activity that will keep us firmly trapped in the prison of our thoughts.

At the same time, it is all very well saying that we simply need to be aware of the content of consciousness, or the experience of being, without judgement, commentary or analysis. That is true. But it is easier said than done, which is why at least some degree of concentration is generally seen as the foundation of any meditation practice. There is a world of difference between watching the thoughts as a detached observer and drifting along within them. Observing one's thoughts—just letting them come and go, without getting involved—takes discipline and practice. Most of the time we are so completely identified with our thoughts that we find it almost impossible to let them go. This is why trying to prac-

tise mindful awareness without an element of focussed attention may well turn out to be indistinguishable from
daydreaming, which is not the same thing as meditation at all.
Conversely, trying too hard to focus the attention, without at
the same time letting go of our thoughts, may result in more
busyness of mind, not less.

This reveals a fundamental paradox that appears to lie at
the heart of meditation, for it seemingly requires us to hold
on and to let go at the same time. On the one hand we are to
keep the mind present by focussing our attention on a single
object and, on the other, we are to cultivate pure awareness by
letting our thoughts come and go without getting caught up in
them. But this is not really a paradox at all, because we avoid
getting caught up in our thoughts precisely by keeping the
mind present. The practice of some kind of mental concentration, such as paying attention to the breathing, is intended as
an anchor for the mind, a way of keeping the mind steady in
order that it may become clear, calm and free from distraction.
It is as if we are distracting the mind from its distractions,
giving it one thing to think about in order to keep it from
thinking about everything else.

So, at the same time as anchoring the attention to the
object of meditation, we also try to let our thoughts, sensations and experiences simply pass by, without getting involved
in the story, without engaging in commentary and evaluation,
without identifying with those thoughts as I, me, or mine. We
cannot stop thoughts from arising, because that's just the
mind doing what it does; but we can step back from the sense
of being the thinker, or subject, of our thoughts, and instead
watch the flow of consciousness as a detached observer. We
can let go of the notion of being the star of the movie in our
mind. This is how we cultivate the sense of serene equanimity
that sees things clearly, as they are in themselves—without
value judgements, commentary or analysis—rather than as *we*

think they should or shouldn't be. Seeing things as they are is the first step towards understanding our conditioning and then being free to choose how we act, rather than always and only ever reacting blindly. Being truly, fully, aware of things as they are, present to reality as it is, is profoundly liberating. In short, by being present, we are living life to the full, as opposed to going through life on autopilot, as if we're not really there at all, caught up in fantasies of past and future, oblivious to what's actually going on right in front of us.

For all the emphasis on meditation technique and practise, it's also important to remember that it is not so much something we do as something we allow to happen. We cannot, by an act of will, make the mind calm, or stop the mind from thinking, for that would involve us in yet more thinking. We can't *stop* thoughts. But we can choose not to get involved in them; we can avoid feeding them with our attention. By just watching thoughts come and go, without getting caught up in them, we can be a little detached from them, at least to some extent. Sometimes the flow might even slow down a bit. With practise it gets easier to observe the mind, to watch the thoughts pass by, like clouds on a gentle breeze. Sometimes we may see that behind the clouds there is clear, empty sky, and that behind the thoughts there is pure, infinite consciousness.

A SIMPLE PRACTICE

To meditate is to abide in the simple awareness of being, just as it is. But this takes practice, because most of the time we are so caught up in the great daydream we call everyday life that we are anything but present to things as they are. That's why we refer to meditation as a discipline, a form of training. Like any other skill, it is something to which we need to apply ourselves—and with which we need to persevere—if we are to gain any benefit from it. But it's also important to remember that we don't practise meditation in order to be really good at meditating, any more than we go to a gym in order to be really good at using exercise machines. We use exercise machines in order to maintain a level of physical fitness that will allow us to do the things we want to do. Similarly, we meditate in order to see things more clearly, live life more skilfully, and become a better version of ourselves, free of those things that, like a lack of physical fitness, drag us down or hold us back.

Not only do we need to avoid the temptation of trying to be good at meditation, we also need to stop worrying about not being good at it! Unfortunately, both of these tendencies are encouraged by almost everything we are likely to read or hear about meditation. Breathless accounts of the benefits we will gain, the blissful states of consciousness we will reach— as long as we do it right—encourage us to adopt a goal-oriented mentality that is bound to end in disappointment. I cannot count the number of times I have heard people say they are 'not very good' at meditation. And there are even more people who think they can't do it at all. This is nonsense, of course. Pretty much everyone can do it because it requires nothing more of us than simply to *be*. What could be easier? The problem is not lack of ability but unrealistic expectations. If we are expecting to become enlightened after one session then the chances are we are going to be disappointed, thinking it's all a waste of time and that we're no good at it. I've been meditating since my twenties and I can't honestly say I'm any 'better' at it now than I was when I started all those years ago. In some ways I may even be 'worse' at it, if—for example—my 'proficiency' is measured by how long I can sit cross-legged on the floor. But, of course, that would be to miss the point entirely. We don't meditate in order to be really good at sitting still and observing our breathing; we meditate in order to cultivate awareness.

Yet, again and again, I hear people apologising for not being any 'good' at meditation, for not being able to sit still, not being able to achieve perfect unwavering concentration. There is no such thing as being good or not good at meditation; there are no degrees of success or failure. Either we are meditating or we are not. Moreover, meditation is not a transaction or a technology, whereby doing it correctly will automatically produce a certain result. It is a process, and a long— quite possibly endless—one at that. We are all beginners and remain so whether we have many years' experience behind us or have just attended a class for the first time. That said, repeated practise, the reinforcement of those positive habits, does help, does make it easier to apply the fruits of our learning to the business of everyday life. But we will still be starting again at the beginning every time we sit and, during a sitting, every time the mind wanders.

Luckily, meditation is something that almost anybody can do. Moreover, nearly everybody who tries it gains some positive benefit from doing so. Even just one session can make you feel calmer and more relaxed afterwards. Those who persevere often find that it contributes to a happier, healthier life – in all sorts of ways. Hopefully, if we stick at it, we will learn to see things more clearly and thereby grow in awareness, which in turn will make us better people and the world around us a better place.

BODY, BREATH AND MIND

When I run training courses to enable people to facilitate Just Meditation sessions, I repeatedly ask a simple question, over and over again. What does someone *need* to know in order to be able to meditate? What is the minimum but sufficient information required by someone who has never meditated before that will allow them to get started? And I encourage them to think this through again and again. Because there are lots of things we *could* say about how to meditate. Far too much, in fact, to include in any one session. And, at the same time, it's easy to make assumptions if we've been meditating for a while, with the result that we don't say enough. At the very first meditation class I ever attended the only instruction given was 'okay, start meditating now'. For anyone with a regular practice that might have been sufficient but, as a complete beginner, I hadn't a clue what I was meant to do! So, what is enough? Or to put it another way, what is the basic minimum someone needs to know in order to be able to do what I'm doing?

The answer is there is something we need to say about the body, and how and where to sit. There is something we need to say about the breath, and its use as a focus for our attention. And there is something we need to say about the mind, and the distracting thoughts we will inevitably experience. In terms of the Just Meditation approach, that's about it. Body, breath and mind. These three dimensions of our existence—namely, the physical, the vital and the mental—constitute the reality of being human. This is the arena in which we are to work at overcoming all that makes us feel trapped and frustrated. It is in body, breath and mind—because it couldn't be anywhere else—that we develop calmness, clarity and compassion.

In considering the body, we are considering our attitude to meditation, in the fullest sense of the word. That is, not only our physical posture but also the location in which our meditation practice takes place. In thinking about the breath, we are addressing the specific object of meditation, the basic method or technique that we use in order to develop calmness and clarity. This may also include the repetition of a mantra or prayer word either instead of, or as well as, focussing our attention on the breathing. And in reflecting on the mind, we are looking more particularly at what we may learn from watching our thoughts and how this leads to the cultivation of awareness.

Meditation can, in theory, be practised anytime and anywhere. But when it comes to 'formal' practise sessions, it usually helps to choose a time and a place that is quiet and where you are unlikely to be disturbed or interrupted. It is not essential to meditate in a location that is completely silent. If it were, very few of us would do any meditating at all. But it does help, especially when starting out, to be in an environment that is reasonably peaceful.

Sit comfortably, either in a chair or on the floor, in such a way that you feel you can remain still for as long as you intend to meditate—whether that be ten minutes, or half an hour—without needing to move around or change position unnecessarily. It will be much easier for our minds to settle down and be still if we can keep ourselves physically still as well. If possible, though it is not essential, try to sit with your back straight and unsupported, in a posture that feels both alert and relaxed at the same time.

You can have your eyes closed, or you can leave them open. Most people usually find it easier to meditate with their eyes closed, but if you prefer to keep your eyes open, just pick a spot somewhere on the floor in front of you and rest your gaze there.

One of the easiest ways to meditate is by using the simple, natural, bodily experience of breathing in and breathing out as something on which to focus your attention. Don't try and breathe in any particular way, or try to control the breath. Just breathe normally—neither fast nor slow—keeping your attention focussed on the experience of simply breathing in and simply breathing out. You may be able to feel the breath at the tip of your nose, and notice the coolness of the air tickling your nostrils. You may be able to feel it in your abdomen as your chest rises and falls with each inhalation and exhalation. Whether focusing the attention on a particular aspect of the breath, or the experience of breathing more generally, just be aware—without thinking about it, without adding commentary and analysis—that as you breathe in you are breathing in, and that as you breathe out you are breathing out.

Keep your attention focussed on the breath. This is easier said than done. Just because we have decided to focus our attention on one thing, it doesn't mean all the other thoughts will simply stop. They won't. The mind will continue to generate thoughts, because that's just what it does. Thoughts of the past, thoughts of the future. And the attention will almost certainly wander. When it does, don't worry. It's normal. It's what happens. But when you notice that your attention has been stolen away and your mind has drifted off into some train of thought or fantasy, when you realise that's what's happened, at that moment your attention has in fact returned to the present. So take it as an opportunity gently but firmly to bring your attention back to the breath, back to the simple experience of being in the here and now. And carry on breathing in and breathing out...

Some people find it helpful to use a prayer word or mantra to help anchor their attention and keep the mind from wandering. Both techniques function in a similar way; the choice of which to use is simply a matter of personal preference. Some prefer to use the breath, others prefer to use a mantra, and many like to combine both together by repeating a mantra in time with the breathing. A word or phrase of two syllables is often recommended, as this can more easily be coordinated with the breath.

In spite of what is sometimes supposed, meditation is not about trying to stop the mind from thinking. Instead, as thoughts arise—which they will, because processing mental data, in other words, thinking, is what the mind does—don't try to suppress them, as this will only generate more thoughts. Simply be aware of the thought, or the feeling it engenders—notice it—but without getting caught up in whatever it is, without engaging in the commentary and analysis. Try instead to cultivate a certain degree of cool detachment. Step back from being the star of the movie in your mind. Just sit and watch the thoughts come and go, without getting involved in the story, quietly observing them as they pass by like leaves floating on a river.

And breathe in and breathe out.

PART II

HOW TO MEDITATE

WE ARE A BODY

There is a widespread, deeply rooted, popular belief that the human person comprises at least two distinct parts. A body, and a mind or soul. Furthermore, these two dimensions of human experience are often considered to be not only fundamentally different, but entirely separable. Some go even further than this, supposing that what we 'really' are is a soul, the body being merely some sort of temporary vessel. Whilst there may be some ways in which such a view makes sense, for most practical purposes it seems enormously unhelpful. The person we are could not be the person we are if it were not the body it is. We do not just *have* a body; we *are* a body. Dismissing the significance of the physical is just as nonsensical as the view that there is nothing but the physical.

Body and mind are an integrated whole, and although meditation is primarily described and experienced as a mental activity, it is not a disembodied or exclusively mental exercise, but one that is situated in the context of our bodily experience. After all, if you think about it, the content of the mind derives from the interaction of our bodily senses with a physical world. Without a body, and its sense organs, there would be nothing for a mind to think. The notion that we could have one without the other, and still fully be the person we are, is completely incoherent.

The body is not just something we 'inhabit', like a set of clothes. That way of thinking only leads back to the dualistic thinking that seeks to separate body and mind. And in the context of meditation, the body is not simply, something we need to put into the right posture so that we can get on with meditation proper. It has a more active role to play in our practice than that. After all, much of what we experience in our minds as we sit and observe the content of consciousness will be directly related to our bodily experience. There will be sounds, there will be sensations; memories of things that have happened, and plans for things we want to do. And of course the breath, as the object of our concentration, is a physical, bodily activity. In other words, the body is the field of our awareness. In fact, it is the only source of awareness we have.

As well as being the site in which experience is experienced, the body can also be an object of meditation in itself. We may find the experience of physical stillness to be so profound that it leads to a deep sense of inner tranquillity, such that we even lose awareness of bodily sensation altogether. People often report not being able to feel parts of their body in meditation: an experience that can either be quite unsettling or rather pleasant, and sometimes even both at the same time. We may also experience pains and discomforts, or other types of unpleasant sensation, of which we might instinctively wish to rid ourselves. Sometimes, however, by choosing instead to sit with the experience, we may find that even painful or unpleasant sensations will very often simply dissipate, leaving us to wonder what that experience, which seemed so real, actually consisted in after all. The body, as the site of all our conscious experience, is thus an important arena for meditation. We can learn a great deal about how our mind works simply by observing the comings and goings of our own experiences, and seeing that these experiences are, like all things, transient and not, ultimately, who and what we really are.

POSTURE

Meditation is sometimes described as simply 'sitting', and in many ways, that is quite apt. Indeed, most of the time that may be the only thing one is actually 'doing' when meditating. There are various ways that one can sit, and one's preference will depend on a variety of personal factors, including age, physical condition, customary habits and so on. The basic options, however, are either to sit on the floor, whether cross-legged or kneeling, or to sit on a chair.

Sitting cross-legged on the floor is the archetypal meditation pose, whether in the full lotus position, or some other posture, either with or without a cushion for extra comfort and support. There are many advantages to sitting like this, for those who are able to, not least because one can do it almost anywhere. It is entirely self-sufficient and requires no additional props or furniture. An alternative to sitting cross-legged is kneeling, usually with the aid of some sort of kneeling bench, which is a posture that is sometimes adopted by those who may have learnt or practised meditation within a Christian context. Of course, it is not possible for everybody to sit in these positions comfortably, and if one is not physically comfortable it will be much more difficult to achieve any degree of mental calm. In most western societies people are not accustomed to sitting on the floor for any length of time, and many will probably find it easier to meditate sitting in a chair. If so, it is best to choose a fairly upright chair, and to sit with your feet firmly planted flat on the ground and your back straight. Tempting as your favourite armchair or sofa might be, it may not necessarily be the best place to meditate.

Some people like to meditate lying down, and this may be appealing, particularly if one's meditation practice has a particular focus on relaxation. The disadvantage is that one is more likely to fall asleep! There is nothing wrong with sleeping, of course, and if we are tired that might be the most appropriate thing to do. But in spite of some similarities between certain states of mind in meditation and the experience of being semi-conscious—half awake and half asleep at the same time—they are not really quite the same thing at all. A little nap might be a pleasant and relaxing experience, but it is not meditation, which necessarily implies a conscious intention. That said, feeling more relaxed is an almost universal effect of meditation, and unsurprisingly therefore, it is quite common for people to become drowsy or even to doze off when trying to meditate. Sitting up straight with the back unsupported can help, and if one is very drowsy—yet determined to stay awake—keeping the eyes open for a bit may help too. Usually, the drowsiness will pass. If one is really tired, however, it might make more sense to take a rest. If meditation is about awareness, then one of the first things we can do is pay more attention to what our body is telling us.

People sometimes wonder whether they should have their eyes open or closed for meditation. Opinions vary, but it doesn't really matter either way. Most people prefer to meditate with their eyes closed, as they find it less distracting and easier to concentrate that way. But some prefer to keep their eyes open, resting their gaze on a fixed point somewhere in front of them. It is just a matter of personal preference, and may depend on a variety of factors. For example, some people might have a particularly vivid imagination that runs riot as soon as they close their eyes. In such circumstances, keeping the eyes open can make it easier to focus the attention on the meditation object.

It is common to see pictures of people holding their hands in particular ways when they meditate, often with palms upright and the thumb touching the tip of the first finger. This is a type of *mudra*, or ritual gesture, which is common to both Hindu and Buddhist traditions. There are many mudras. Most just involve the hands, but some take in other parts of the body too. Mudras play an important part in traditional yoga, where they are used to stimulate certain psychic or physiological processes, as well as being a prominent feature of classical Indian dance. Statues or images of the Buddha will often incorporate various mudras, depending on the particular symbolism being conveyed. The recommendation here, as with all things, is to keep it simple. One can either have the hands on the knees, palms up or down, or one can just hold them loosely together in the lap. It doesn't really matter how we hold our hands. What is more important is that it feels natural and relaxed, and that it becomes part of the way you routinely sit for meditation.

Whatever posture we choose to adopt—whether sitting on the floor or in a chair—it is essential that we are comfortable, so it can be helpful to begin a session by mentally scanning through the body to make sure we are properly relaxed, and not holding any tension in our muscles. I usually recommend that, if possible, people should try and sit with their back straight and unsupported, with hands resting on the knees or loosely held together in their lap, in a posture that feels both alert and relaxed at the same time. Of course, this is not always feasible for everybody. Back pain or a host of other ailments may prevent us from sitting in a 'proper' meditation posture. The main thing is to try and find a position that feels reasonably comfortable and free from tension, wherever and whatever that may be for us. If the aim of meditation is to achieve stillness of mind, we will find this much easier if we can also establish an equivalent stillness in the body. If we want the mind to be calm and attentive, then we should adopt a meditation posture that will somehow reflect and reinforce this intention.

LOCATION

As bodies, we occupy space. Therefore, some consideration should also be given to the place and environment in which we choose to meditate. Clearly, this is a matter in which individual circumstances will vary considerably. Some people might be able to allocate a whole room in their house solely for use as a meditation space, where they are able to create an environment specially designed to support their practice. Most will probably have to manage with spaces that may feel less than perfect in some way or other. We have to make the best of the circumstances in which we find ourselves, and accept that the extent to which we are able to determine the external conditions of our practice may be limited. This is, of course, one reason why people attend classes and retreats in places specifically intended to accommodate meditation practice. But if we really want to make meditation part of our daily life, then we might want to consider trying to establish a dedicated spot at home – if we haven't already done so. Even if it is no more than a particular chair or a corner of a room that we use, we can still make this our regular meditation space.

We will also want to make sure that the time and place we choose for our meditation practice is one that is unlikely to be disturbed. This may sometimes be difficult if we share our home with others, especially young children. But if we are serious about wanting to meditate then we may need to make some little adjustments to our routine or domestic arrangements in order to give ourselves the space we need, both literally and figuratively. It can also be helpful to try and stick to the same time and place, in as much as that is possible, so that we cultivate positive habits that reinforce our practice. Making meditation part of a regular routine, sitting at the same time and in the same place, and adopting the same posture each time we meditate, creates a 'body memory', which automatically gets us into a meditative frame of mind whenever we sit for our meditation practice. It is not essential to have the perfect environment for meditation—and we should be wary of allowing the lack of ideal conditions to become an excuse not to practise—but anything we can do to make our circumstances more conducive to meditation will obviously enhance our efforts.

THE BREATH OF LIFE

If the practice of meditation, simply stated, entails focussing the mind on one thing, whilst at the same time trying to avoid getting caught up in thinking about other things, then one of the most basic, most common—and most effective—meditation techniques involves a conscious intention to anchor the attention to the simple experience of just breathing in and breathing out. Sometimes known as 'mindfulness of breathing', this—together with the use of a mantra for those who find that helpful—is, in essence, the method that I am calling 'Just Meditation'. The use of the breath as an object of meditation is arguably the most widespread of techniques, and can be found in both eastern and western spiritual traditions. Its universal appeal may be attributed to a number of factors, including its simplicity, as well as the rich symbolism associated with the breath itself.

One of the principal advantages of using the breath as our focus for meditation is that it is a natural bodily process, which just happens automatically without us having to remember to do it. And yet, unlike some of our other bodily functions, such as our heartbeat or the workings of our kidneys, we can also exercise a degree of deliberate control over it. We can choose whether to take rapid breaths, or to breathe more slowly; we can even decide to hold our breath altogether – at least for short periods of time. Indeed the breath is like a bridge between the body and mind. For example, we know from ordinary experience that if we are relaxed, or fully absorbed in some task or activity, our breathing will be slow and steady, whereas if we are nervous or agitated it will be shallow and fast. The breath thus connects the physical with the mental and emotional dimensions of experience, which is why we commonly advise people to 'take a deep breath' when they need to calm down, and also explains why breathing exercises can be such an effective way of helping the mind settle into a more contemplative state. But arguably the most significant feature of the breath as an object of meditation is simply this. The mind is rarely present—it is generally experienced as projections of the past or the future—whereas the body is always and only present: it cannot be anywhere else *but* in the here and now. Therefore, if we can keep the mind anchored to the physical experience of breathing, we may be able to bring it into the reality of the present occupied by the body.

Because the breath represents this profound connection between the spiritual and material dimensions of our being, it tends to be associated with potent symbolism. For example, in the story of creation recorded in the Book of Genesis—which, regardless of what people may variously think about the 'truth' of it, has nevertheless shaped our understanding of the human condition for over two millennia—when God creates Adam and Eve he breathes the breath of life into them. The Latin word for breath, *spiritus*, gives us the notion of the soul or spirit as the essence of our being, an essence that is somehow also connected to the divine, or that which is ultimately real and true. As the animating spirit of life within us, the breath is a symbol of the universal energy that pervades the whole of existence. Our breath is what we share with one another and thus what we have in common with all that is. And as one of our vital signs it is an indicator that we are alive. But the insubstantiality of the breath also alerts us to the fragile contingency of existence: life really is as ephemeral as a puff of air. By using the breath as an object of meditation, we signify the intimate connection between body and spirit, and between us as individuals and the cosmos of which we are a part. By the simple act of focussing our attention on the breath we somehow connect with and abide in the deepest reality of what we are.

Used as an object of meditation, the breath serves as something on which to focus the attention, an anchor to steady the mind and discourage it from wandering. As we watch and breathe, we try to keep our attention focussed on the simple, natural experience of the breath coming in and the breath going out. We may wish to concentrate our attention on a particular spot, such as the tip of our nose. We may be able to notice the sensation of the air in our nostrils. We may wish to focus on the feeling of the breath in our body as our chest rises and falls with each inhalation and exhalation. Or we may simply be aware of the fact that as we breathe in we are breathing in, and as we breathe out we are breathing out.

Although the aim is just to breathe naturally, and be aware of the breath without analysing it or even thinking about it at all, there are one or two additional things we can do with the breath to increase its usefulness in meditation. For example, sometimes when settling in to begin a period of meditation, it may help to take a couple of deep breaths, in order to get centred and make us more fully aware of the breath in our present-moment experience. It is also possible to reinforce our concentration on the breath by counting, which can be especially helpful when the mind is very restless. There are a number of ways of doing this, but one of the simplest exercises is to count up to ten, in time with the breathing. In other words, as you breathe in, mentally count one, as you breathe out, mentally count one; breathe in count two, breathe out count two, and so on, up to ten. And then, if you like, you can count the breaths back down to one again. If you lose count, or forget where you've got to, start over at one again. If you suddenly realise you've counted up to thirty-four, start back at one again! It can sometimes be helpful to do this exercise at the start of a session, perhaps just once up to ten and then back down again, as a way of settling the mind, before continuing with just observing the breath as normal.

Meditation on the breath is very simple at one level, but at the same time it can be a lot harder than it sounds. I can remember once attending a talk given by a Tibetan Buddhist teacher who wagered that we would not be able to meditate for even just three breaths without being distracted. To my amazement, I found it was almost impossible to maintain concentration for more than a few seconds at a time, if that. It is extremely difficult to keep the mind entirely and exclusively focussed on one thing only. The tiniest lapse in concentration will be more than sufficient to allow other thoughts to make themselves present, and as soon as we start thinking about something else, that's it. Meditation over. But that's okay. When we realise our attention has wandered, we take that as an opportunity to bring the attention back to the breath. Noticing we have become distracted is arguably even a good thing: it indicates that our awareness has returned to the present. The difficulty is keeping it there. So, we need to have the presence of mind to start again, gently but firmly bringing the attention back to the breath, back to the here and now. And just carry on breathing in and breathing out...

In spite of the very widespread use of the breath as an object of meditation, it is not always the most suitable method for everyone. There are many people for whom breathing might be difficult at the best of times, perhaps due to asthma or other respiratory conditions, and focussing on it may have the adverse effect of emphasising those difficulties. Rather than helping to calm the mind, trying to concentrate on our breathing may actually cause greater anxiety as we become intensely self-conscious of each breath and maybe even find ourselves struggling to breathe at all. The very fact of this happening could in itself be something to notice and be aware of, and it may be that any tension or anxiety will subsequently subside. But if not, then it would obviously be better to try a different technique. Alongside mindfulness of breathing, another of the most common meditation techniques involves the repetition of a prayer word or mantra, either on its own or synchronised with the breathing. Just as anchoring our attention to the breath gives the mind something to focus on, so in the same way, repeating a single word or phrase over and over again gives the voice in our heads something to say, so that it doesn't chatter away about anything and everything else.

MANTRAS

The term 'mantra' usually refers to a word or phrase that is continually repeated, either as a meditation practice or a devotional exercise. It comes from the Sanskrit root *man-*, from which we derive various terms related to mental phenomena and the act of thinking. Mantras come in all shapes and sizes, and can consist of almost anything from a single syllable to several sentences. They can be meaningless phonetic sounds —not even actual words at all—or they can be whole prayers or hymns imbued with profound meaning and significance.

Broadly speaking, there are two ways in which mantras are used: either as part of a meditation technique, or as a form of prayer or devotion – or both at the same time. When used as an object of meditation, a mantra is a word or phrase that is repeated over and over again in order to give the mind just one thought to think. Used in this way, a mantra provides a focus for the attention—in a similar way to being mindful of the breath—intended to prevent the mind from getting caught up in all the other thoughts that will otherwise steal our attention away. As an aid to concentration, a way of keeping the mind from wandering by anchoring it to a single object of awareness, the meaning of the mantra is often irrelevant. Any word, sound, or series of words will do. It is simply a verbal utterance on which to focus our attention so that the mind doesn't distractedly babble on about other things.

There are also various expressions of mantra meditation in which the use of the mantra is understood as rather more than just a word or sound to help focus the mind: the mantra is significant in itself. In some traditions, for example, it is maintained that the sonic vibration of a particular mantra will have some sort of specific effect on the person repeating it, or that the mantra should be chosen by matching its vibration to the unique vibration of the individual soul. Then there are those traditions of mantra meditation where the repetition of the sacred word or sound is understood as a form of prayer or divine invocation, perhaps of the name of God, which—by being repeated—is believed to activate or release the divine energy that the word represents. If this seems a bit mysterious, think about the way in which the repetition of a simple phrase, such as 'thank you', can engender in the mind the actual feeling and experience of gratitude that the words represent. Language plays a part in actually shaping, not merely describing, reality as we experience it. Thus the meaning of a word can become manifest in the consciousness of the one who repeats it.

When using a mantra or prayer word as an aid to meditation, and especially if it is intended that the repetition of it should be coordinated with the breathing, I would always recommend a word or phrase of two syllables, as this can more easily be synchronised with the breath. There are some examples of two-syllable mantras listed in the glossary. It doesn't have to be a word or phrase that means anything. Indeed, some people prefer to use a mantra that has no obvious meaning at all, on the assumption that we are less likely to be distracted by thinking about all the connotations which that word or phrase may possess. Others, however, prefer their mantra to mean something significant, or to communicate a specific value. It doesn't really make much difference either way; it's really just a matter of personal preference and what works best for us. The important thing is that once we have found a mantra that feels right, we should stick with it. Whether mantras are used as a simple aid to concentration, or with some other intention, repetition helps to reinforce the practice. Over time, we may find that our mantra may even start to repeat itself automatically, accompanying us as we go about our daily business, and this will help us build a mindful attitude into everyday life.

WHOSE MIND IS IT ANYWAY

There comes a point in everyone's life, probably sometime during childhood, when we realise that we are constantly talking to ourselves. There is a voice in our heads giving a non-stop running commentary on life, a narrator telling the story of our life in the form of an endless monologue made up of memories, fantasies, imagined conversations, plans, regrets, hopes, fears and lots of random nonsense. The voice in our heads is always there, whether awake or asleep (the latter is what we call dreaming). It is a perfectly natural consequence of self-awareness, which is to say that as human beings, we are not only conscious of our experience—as are many other animals—but we also have the ability to reflect on it objectively.

Our capacity for abstract reflection is essentially what we refer to as the mind. Much of the time we may not be particularly aware of this voice; we're too busy getting on with life. But when we pause for a moment, or take a step back from actively doing stuff—such as when we meditate—we are likely to become much more aware of the constant burble of commentary, judgement, evaluation and analysis going on in our heads, all the time. This commentary, on the world and the people around us, is completely normal, of course, but it also creates a subtle barrier that separates us from reality as it is. Our perceptions of things are not the things themselves. Moreover, the voice in our heads can also sometimes descend into a deeply negative habit of constant criticism, of everyone and everything, a tendency that has been described in the Christian contemplative tradition as 'murmuring'.

Originally derived from the Bible stories of the Israelites in the wilderness, who were constantly complaining about their predicament, murmuring is essentially the unconscious habit we have of making judgements, mostly unfavourable, about others in comparison with ourselves. It manifests as all the little disparaging comments we make. It is our propensity for gossip, slander, backstabbing and snide remarks. Murmuring occurs not only when we are explicitly grumbling aloud about everything that is wrong with the world; it is also present in our thoughts. We are murmuring when we privately criticise or find fault with other people—or ourselves, for that matter —commenting on their behaviour or even just their appearance. We are murmuring whenever we complain about how things would be so much better if only they were done my way. Indeed, if we listen carefully to our internal commentary, especially when we're not really thinking about anything in particular, we will find that good deal of it consists of unguarded, capricious murmuring. Murmuring is not the expression of a justifiable grievance, or respectful disagreement, but something altogether more insidious: it is a sign of profound discontent, which very often manifests as an attempt to justify our behaviour by attributing our own faults and failings to others. Murmuring is the corrosive, poisonous whispering that prevents us from truly listening to each other, and it is something that we all do, all the time. Left unchecked, murmuring can easily become an all-pervasive censorious attitude to everything, which entrenches us in ruts of negativity and sours our relationships – with the world, with other people and with ourselves.

Murmuring is in many ways the opposite of being mindful. And it comes so naturally to us that most of the time we are not even aware that we are doing it – let alone how toxic and destructive it can be. If we make an effort to be aware of it, however, we are likely to find ourselves murmuring in our ordinary everyday conversation, as we grumble and complain about things or make disapproving comments about other people. We will notice that the voice in our heads is very often engaged in murmuring of one sort or another and, most of all, we will find ourselves murmuring as we try to meditate. When we become aware that we are murmuring in meditation, we should, as always, simply acknowledge the thought for what it is—without applying further judgement or evaluation—and let it go. If we can learn to be more mindful during those times we deliberately set aside to practise, we may also learn to become more aware of our habitual murmuring as we are going about our daily business. By becoming more mindful of our thoughts and words—and their impact on others—our meditation practice will extend into, and thereby transform, the whole of life.

The problem, however, is that we are for the most part so absorbed in our self-centred preoccupations and so caught up in our internal commentary on life—in other words, murmuring—that we are only rarely present to the reality of things in front of us, or the other people around us. How can we be truly listening to life if there is a voice in our heads that is already doing all the talking, distracting us from the here and now, superimposing a layer of commentary and interpretation on reality, and preventing us from being present to the world and one another? How can we expect to see things as they really are if we are unable to see beyond the little bubble of our own personal perceptions and projections? How do we imagine we will be able to connect with others if we are constantly complaining about them; if our ego keeps getting in the way? Taken to the extreme, murmuring can become such an obstacle to genuine interaction between people that it will contaminate the life of any community, undermine the fundamental relationships that sustain it, and eventually destroy it altogether.

This voice in our heads is the principal way in which we experience the flow of consciousness that we call the mind. Our thoughts are, generally speaking, articulated in language. Even those thoughts that may be experienced in predominantly visual or auditory forms will usually be accompanied by some form of verbal commentary or labelling. Whilst this is perfectly natural—it's just the mind doing what it does—it can become a problem when we act on the assumption that we really are the story we tell, when we see the world in terms of our projections, when we mistake our commentary for reality, rather than seeing things as they are. And it is problematic because that disjunction between things as they are and things as we think they should or shouldn't be lies at the root of so much of the stress, anxiety, frustration and negativity that we experience in life. But if we can at least start to see this, we may be able to take a first step towards being free of it.

Whilst meditation is certainly about taking a step back from the commentary, and not identifying with the voice in our heads, it is not—as we have to keep reminding ourselves —about trying to stop the mind from thinking. If only that were possible! Thoughts will continue to be generated by the mind as long as there is breath in the body, because that is what the mind is: the constant murmuring flow of consciousness. Therefore, as thoughts arise—which they will—do not try to suppress them, as this only generates more thoughts.

Simply try not to get caught up in the story; try to step back from the notion of being the star of the movie in your mind. Rather than identify as the subject of those thoughts, which come and go of their own accord without any need of a 'thinker', just be aware of them as they arise and as they disappear, quietly observing the stream of consciousness as if sitting on a river bank watching the water flow past.

Needless to say, this is easier said than done. We identify with our thoughts. We think of ourselves in terms of our memories and speculations, our hopes, fears, ideas and emotions. We construct our sense of self from our thoughts, thereby creating the notion of the one who thinks those thoughts, even though, when we think about it, we discover that in fact the thinker is just another thought. Who we are is just what we think we are and, like everything else, that too comes and goes. And yet such is the power of this flow of consciousness to captivate our attention that it is all but impossible not to get caught up and swept away by it. But we are not our thoughts. If anything, we are the flow of consciousness, but instead we make the mistake of clinging to and identifying with some particular element within it—a thought, in other words—which is then taken as being I, me or mine. The idea that there is a self that is somehow the 'driver' of the 'vehicle' that is 'me' is compelling, but also quite possibly an illusion. We have no control over our body, and whether it gets sick or remains healthy. We have even less control over the mind and what it thinks, as demonstrated by the fact that whenever we try not to think of something, that very something is exactly what comes to mind! How are we to take a step back from our thoughts when we imagine that we are the thoughts themselves?

The good news is that the mind can only think one thought at a time. It is a linear processor. We may have the experience, sometimes, of our minds being so busy that we seem to be thinking of all sorts of different things at the same time, but this is an illusion created by the mind's ability to jump very rapidly back and forth between different thoughts. In any given moment of consciousness, however, we think only one thought at a time. It therefore stands to reason that if the mind can stay focussed on one single thought, then it will not be distracted by all the other thoughts. The practice of meditation is to try and keep the attention on one thought—such as awareness of the breath—whilst letting all the other thoughts simply pass by, without getting involved and caught up in them, without becoming the 'thinker' of our thoughts.

THOUGHTS

W hat is a thought? It might seem like a strange question. A thought is, well, something we think, obviously. But that doesn't really provide us with an answer. What, *exactly*, are thoughts? What is the unit of consciousness? What is 'mind stuff'? There is something we call thinking. There are conscious experiences we call thoughts. And there are some of these with which we are so closely identified that we literally become them. We call these experiences 'feelings'. Sometimes we feel our feelings so strongly that they become more than merely mental experiences; they are actually felt physically. Strong emotions—such as fear, anger or desire—can all be felt in the body as well being experienced in the mind. So if we want to avoid getting caught up in our thoughts, if we want sometimes to be able to let them go, then it might help if we can see them more clearly and understand them for what they are.

At the most fundamental level thoughts are composed of perceptions, that is, basic units of mental data obtained from our sensory faculties. If we examine our thoughts carefully, we will discover that any complex thought can be seen to comprise bits of primary information, that must at one time or other have been acquired through the senses. Everything we experience, in every moment of consciousness, is registered as a simple unit of mental information. And we are, of course, receiving a vast amount of sensory information in every single moment of consciousness; often far more than we can actually process or be aware of at the time. These bits of raw data are then compounded to produce the complex mental phenomena we call thoughts. It is a process analogous to the way in which individual letters of the alphabet can be arranged in an infinite variety of different configurations to produce an infinite variety of words, which in turn can be combined into an infinite variety of sentences, and so on. We can even create sentences that are grammatically correct but don't mean anything – and *vice versa*. All the thoughts, feelings and ideas we have, even abstract concepts, can thus be reduced to permutations of basic bits of primary data, all of it derived in one way or another from our senses.

If we can slow the mind down, and step back from the notion of being the thinker in order to look at these individual sense impressions, we may notice that each bit of information automatically engenders a feeling response that is somehow either positive or negative, and which we experience in terms of a feeling of attraction or aversion. Just to be clear, when we talk about feelings here, we do not mean those complex emotional states we usually refer to when we talk about feelings, such as love or grief, joy or despair, empathy or envy, guilt, hope, anger or kindness. The word 'feelings' in this context refers simply to the basic instinctive reactions to each and every piece of sensory data that is received and recorded by our consciousness. A sound, or a touch; a taste or a sight. Each impression, whatever it may be, is automatically evaluated as being in some way positive, or in some way negative. Thus, each sense impression, each bit of mental data, each basic experience is assessed as agreeable or disagreeable, pleasant or unpleasant, and then labelled and filed accordingly.

This process of evaluating our experience in either positive or negative terms is what ultimately gives rise to the sense of identification with the phenomena of experience as being I, me, or mine. In other words, the labelling of any given experience or perception as being either positive or negative gives rise to a feeling of attraction or aversion that automatically implies a subject that wants to own or disown the experience in question. If labelled positive, we will be attracted towards it, we will want to prolong or increase it; if negative, we will experience aversion, we will want to reduce or avoid it. And whilst this is a completely natural process, which has its part to play in enabling us to get on with normal life, the problem comes when we mistake our projections for reality, when we imagine ourselves to be what we are not. My thoughts about the world do not necessarily reflect the way the world really is. My value judgements, and the commentary in my head, do not reflect things as they are but as I think they should or shouldn't be. Thus the 'non-judgemental awareness' we hear about in connection with the cultivation of mindfulness is the practice of simply being aware of the content of consciousness, without evaluating it and thereby identifying with it as I, me, or mine.

Thoughts are just mental data, but thinking would appear to imply a 'thinker'. This is where it starts to get really interesting, because when we ask ourselves who or what is this 'I' who is the thinker of my thoughts, who apparently has will and intention, it is very difficult to say. If we start to explore this question, we may find that the notion of an 'I' arises from the natural tendency to evaluate perceptions and consequently to identify with the various thoughts in which the 'I' then features as the subject, or the 'star of the movie'. As we learn to observe the content of consciousness objectively and dispassionately, we can see that in fact these thoughts are not really me, not really mine. Indeed, the very act of seeing 'our' thoughts as objects is automatically to see them as other than the seeing subject. And when we look at that subject, we see another thought that is not really I, me, or mine either. And so on, *ad infinitem*. The 'I' is a construct, a projection of the notion of self onto phenomena that are not truly the 'self' at all. Experiences, sensations, thoughts and feelings come and go of their own accord. They are impersonal, natural processes, which do not require an 'owner'.

Unfortunately, it can be difficult to see that the commentator is itself a product of the commentary; it is hard to see 'our' thoughts as merely streams of random data when we are so closely identified with them. And yet, at the same time, we also know that we are able to experience thoughts that we are not consciously thinking, such as the strange experiences and phantom sensations that sometimes arise in meditation. When the mind is left to idle in neutral it can conjure up all sorts of stuff, without the need for any corresponding sense of 'me' being the 'thinker'. Thoughts are just churning around in the mind all the time, whether 'we' are consciously thinking them or not. The fact that we can be aware both of thoughts that we are not thinking—dreams would be another example —as well as thoughts that are attached to a sense of an I, would seem to indicate that what we call thinking is an identi- fication of the notion of I, me, mine with thoughts. There is, in truth, no thinker as such; just as there is no fire separate from the fuel that is being burned. What we call fire is the phenomenon of something burning. What we call thinking is the phenomenon of thoughts being identified as I, me and mine. In meditation we let go of all the things that we think of as being I, me and mine. My thoughts, my worries, my plans, my dreams, my hopes, my fears, my pain, my joy. We can be free of the power our thoughts have over us if we do not feed the idea that they must be *mine*.

Whatever we may ordinarily think, our thoughts are simply not our own. If I tell you not to think of an elephant, then that is exactly what will come to mind. You did not choose to think of an elephant, and nor could you have chosen not to think of an elephant. This may be a simplistic illustration, but the point it makes is an important one. We have no control over our thoughts. Indeed, they control us. They think themselves. Thoughts arise, unbidden, and they can't be unthought. But we can, to some extent, direct our attention, and by doing so, we can calm the mind a little, perhaps even enough to be able to observe our thoughts objectively. We can see how they make us feel, we can see where we are in those thoughts. And we can try not to get involved in them. If we cannot control our thoughts, if they just come and go without us even having to think them, if the thinker is just another thought and in a very real sense we are not our thoughts, then we can choose not to let them control us. If we can see our thoughts as objects we might cease to be their subjects.

By learning not to identify with the content of consciousness we may be able to loosen the grip of our conditioning and dismantle our attachments. Using the breath as a focus for our attention, an anchor for the mind, we learn to be aware of reality as it is in the present moment, without getting swept away by fantasies of past and future, without evaluating experience in positive or negative terms. Reality, and our experience of it, is just what it is. In meditation, we strive to understand that when we see, there is just seeing; when we hear, there is just hearing. That is not to say we can't enjoy things, or that we have to put up with discomfort or injustice. It means we enjoy without attachment to outcomes, without grasping for more, accepting that the object of that joy will pass away, without suffering the pain of loss. It means we avoid discomfort, or oppose injustice, acting out of wisdom and compassion, rather than for personal advantage. This is what enables us to eradicate our conditioning, and free ourselves from bondage to the unsatisfactoriness of the human condition and the delusion of being the experiencer of experience. This, in short, is the point of it all.

The sense that we are our thoughts can be almost impossible to shake off. But although we cannot control our thoughts, we can change the way we relate to them. Calm observation and a disciplined intention not to identify with them will expose the fact that even obsessive thoughts are as impermanent as any other, and not who and what we really are. If and when we do manage to detach ourselves from the notion of being the thinker of the thoughts, becoming instead a dispassionate observer of the random stream of consciousness, we may feel we are experiencing something like a waking dream, as the mind continues to churn mental data, producing random images and information. We learn from this that all thoughts come and go, and that our identification with them as being I, me or mine is, fundamentally, an illusion. As we meditate, sitting quietly and observing the constant manipulation of this mental data, we can see each thought in terms of its basic components and simply let them come and go on their own, like leaves dancing in the wind.

PAST AND FUTURE

If we've never really given it much thought, we probably think that we have lots of different kinds of thoughts, but I suggest that all our thoughts can actually be reduced to just two basic categories. All our mental activity, in all its apparent variety, can be seen to consist of either reimagining the past (which has ceased to exist) or speculating about the future (which has yet to exist). In other words, we have only two narrative genres: history and fantasy, vehicles respectively of memory and hope. These two types of thought can be experienced in both positive and negative modes. Thoughts about the past may generate feelings that are pleasant or unpleasant (either of which could be experienced as regret), whilst thoughts about the future can inspire feelings of longing or of dread. Every thought can be classified as one or other of these two basic types, which means that if we are caught up in our thoughts, we are not abiding in the awareness of reality as it is, but floating instead in a fantasy world we have constructed and projected onto the simple truth of what is. Therefore, as thoughts arise in meditation, we may sometimes find it helpful to label them as either memories of things past, or fantasies and speculations about things yet to be. If we can name our thoughts as we become aware of them—as either memory or fantasy, and therefore not in need of our attention *right now*—we may be able to subvert their tendency to steal our attention away from the present, and perhaps find ourselves more able to let them go.

But it's easier said than done. We can be so caught up in our commentary on life that we are rarely, if ever, aware of the experience of being present. Our minds are constantly projecting into the past or the future, but both of these are fantasies. If we are not present, we are not fully engaged with what we're actually doing or what's right in front of us. If we go through life on auto-pilot, we are more than likely going to make mistakes. And all the while life quite literally passes us by. Worse still, we can get trapped in the past or the future, which then becomes a prison that renders us unable to act decisively in the present. There are any number of ways we can be held captive by our past, by the paralysing effects of regret or shame, for example. We talk about people being stuck in the past, unable to move on. And fantasies about the future can be just as debilitating. If we are living in expectation of a particular outcome, waiting impatiently for something to happen—or in fear of what may or may not come to pass—we can be completely incapacitated, unable to function normally because we've convinced ourselves that everything depends on things turning out a certain way.

The crucial point to grasp in all of this is it's not so much that past and future don't presently exist, and that we must try not to think of them in order to be present, but rather that in reality, they *only* exist in the present. When we think of the past, we bring it to mind. It is not really the past, but a representation of the past, as imagined in the present. Likewise our speculations about the future are projections of the future, as imagined in the present. The problem is we get so caught up in the fantasy, that we bypass the present by projecting ourselves into an imagined past or an imagined future and live life through our projections as if they are real, whilst ignoring what is actually present. What we call the mind, then, is the identification of the sense of self with an imagined past or future. The mind, as such, is seldom, if ever, present, so the present is something we rarely experience. We forget the present as we get lost in reverie, rather than being fully and truly present to reality as it is. And yet, in reality there is only the present—even when it presents itself as thoughts of the past or the future—we just have to realise it. Time is, in some sense, an illusion: past and future are both projections, fantasies constructed in the present but at the same time removed from it. They don't really exist. Though we are never present, at the same time, we can only be present, because the time is always now. And yet, as soon as it is here it is gone. The eternal now is intangible, unreal, and—paradoxically—the *only* thing that's real: an infinite potentiality that is both everything there is and nothing at all.

Admittedly it is both natural and necessary to pay a certain amount of attention to the past and the future, to situate ourselves in the context of a past that gives us meaning and in relation to a future that gives us purpose, even if neither are presently real. On the one hand, if we did not have a past we would have no sense of who we are, and on the other, the assumption that we will still exist in the future gives significance to what we do in the present. If we had neither a sense of identity based on our past, nor the ability to assume we had a future, everyday life would be impossible. It takes a certain amount of courage to let all of that go and simply abide in the indeterminate present, as it is, rather than as we think it should or shouldn't be. But that is what we have to do if we want to be free.

DISTRACTIONS

When we meditate, we set a conscious intention to step out of the fantasy of past and future into the reality of the present. But it takes practise. Sometimes the mind is relatively calm and settles down easily. Our thoughts will just drift across our consciousness like clouds gently floating across a summer sky. We will be relatively untroubled by distraction, and we will feel calm and refreshed afterwards. Like muddy water that slowly settles to become clear, so our minds will become clear and we will see things as they really are. We will see that we are not our thoughts; we are not the voice in our heads. Most of the time, however, our minds are restless and distracted, caught up in our thoughts, dragged here and there by the winds of our desires, hopes, fears and regrets. It is estimated that we spend up to half our waking lives daydreaming—drifting aimlessly through fantasy, distraction and speculation—thinking of greener grass or what might have been if only... It is also said that we are least happy when daydreaming like this, which should hardly be surprising. Disengaging from life and spending it in idle reverie leads inevitably to frustration and disappointment.

Sometimes people complain that they cannot meditate because of distractions, especially external noises. However, the truth is that the most distracting distractions are the ones that come from within. As we meditate we may come to see that when we find ourselves distracted by something external to us, the real distraction is not whatever is going on out there in the world around us, but our reaction to it: the voice in our heads that's complaining about being distracted. Rather than blaming the world for distracting us, however, we could more usefully think of distractions as our friends. Meditation is not about having no distractions but learning not to be distracted by them, practising the discipline of deliberately placing our attention elsewhere, rather than just letting ourselves get absorbed by our thoughts. And we'll find it much easier to do that if we can get to know our distractions first. Sometimes, the so-called distraction will be the very thing that reminds us that we weren't actually meditating at all but merely daydreaming. As we become more experienced in meditation, we become more aware of how our mind works and we learn things about ourselves that we might not normally notice. Sometimes distractions can even become aids to our medita-tion. Rather than complaining about a persistent noise, for example, we can choose instead to use it as an object of medi-tation, something on which to focus our listening attention. The same principle can sometimes be applied to physical sensations, even discomfort or pain. If we can't let it go, then sitting with it is the only alternative. And by doing that we may see that it, too, comes and goes. Admittedly, some external distractions are too distracting. For example, music and conversation can be particularly difficult to ignore, or use as a focus for our attention. Instead, we may just have to accept the fact that we are distracted, whilst at the same time learning what we can from being aware of how we react to the experience.

With practise we can learn to let go of the sense of our own involvement in our thoughts, and simply let them come and go of their own accord. But sometimes we just can't seem to get to that point. Sometimes our thoughts are too intense. Sometimes our minds will be so turbulent—with or without the excuse of external distractions—that it is quite impossible to settle and be calm. This may be because there is something forcing itself into our consciousness that needs to be acknowledged or dealt with. It may be that we are anxious about some plans we are making, or a difficult encounter we may have recently had, or may be about to have. We may be troubled by a disturbing memory, or a feeling of anger, shame or disgust, and want to reject or deny it. We may be enticed by an appealing fantasy and experience the feeling of wanting to indulge in it further.

Sometimes things come up during meditation that are difficult for us to sit with, that might make us feel intensely anxious and uncomfortable. Some of our memories may be particularly troubling. I cannot deny that I have done many things of which I am not proud, or that I deeply regret. I have experienced things that caused me a great deal of distress, both at the time and since. And I have caused suffering to those around me and behaved in ways that I would be swift to condemn in others. Like everyone else who has ever lived, I do things I know I shouldn't, and I don't do things I know I should. When we sit for meditation, it is not just possible, but highly likely, that we will be disturbed by all sorts of unwelcome thoughts, memories and feelings. Our instinct is to want to push them away, to repress or avoid such states of mind. But the chances are we will get caught up in them, because of our sense of personal ownership and identification with these experiences, memories or feelings. We won't be able to push them away because the attempt to do so will just get us more tangled up in whatever it is. And that might be hard.

As always, however, the approach remains the same. We note our awareness of the thought, whatever it may be, and we try not to get involved but just let it pass by. We learn to see that we are not our thoughts, and that however unpleasant or disturbing they may be, they are still 'just thoughts'. They will pass. Learning how to do this is what we practise when we practise meditation. However, some thoughts hold us in a firmer grip. Some thoughts are almost impossible to let go. Some thoughts become obsessions that literally possess our minds completely and will not leave us alone but continue to haunt us, for days, months or even years on end. If the thought is strong, if a certain state of mind is more intense, more engaging than the stream of random nonsense that makes up most of our mental activity, if we can't let it go but are very much caught up in whatever it may be, then we should simply be aware of that fact too. If you really can't let a thought go, if it is so nagging and persistent that it won't leave you alone, then don't struggle with it. This is not a mental wrestling match; it's about accepting the reality of reality as it is, rather than as we think it should be or shouldn't be. We cannot change the past or determine the future; but we can decide how we relate to our thoughts, and whether or not we are going to let them control us. So instead of trying to force the thought to leave, welcome it in and have a really good look at it. Try to cultivate a sense of open-minded and objective curiosity towards that thought. What is it about? How does it make you feel? Where has it come from? What does it want from you? Do you want to repress it or indulge it? Does it make you feel joy or fear? Is it an idea you want to resist or encourage? Does it *have* to make you feel that way, or could you feel differently about it?

If we can learn to observe the working of the mind objectively and become aware of feelings of attraction when they arise, or aversion when in turn they arise—and also when they subside and pass away—then we are being mindful, we are growing in awareness, we are learning to see things more clearly. Doing this is to exercise a level of detachment no less significant than letting things go without getting involved in the first place, because to see a thought or feeling as an object automatically dissolves the subjective identification with it as I, me, or mine. And the chances are, it will just disappear anyway – at least for a while. Even in the case of thoughts and memories that may be disturbing or traumatic to recall, we can learn how better to manage our responses. In so doing we will see that the thought, however troubling it may be, is still just a thought, and the feeling it engenders, however unpleasant it may be, is still just a feeling. We may not be able change the things that have happened in our lives, but we can change how we see them and how we feel about them. If we can just sit and watch, we will come to see the process by which thoughts and feelings arise, and the way in which our sense of self is identified with those states of mind. We will also see how they pass away and cease to be, because—like all things—they come and they go.

The cultivation of a calm, tranquil mind, free from distractions and disturbances, resting in serene, focussed awareness of the reality of the present as it is in itself, rather than as we think it should or shouldn't be, is what we are trying to 'achieve' in meditation. By simply observing the content of consciousness with dispassionate equanimity, we learn how to ignore our distractions and see things as they really are, thereby gaining valuable insight into the truth, both of ourselves and the other people with whom we share our world. This enables us to live life more skilfully. Therefore, meditation, the cultivation of awareness—or calmness, clarity and compassion—is simply the observation of thoughts, feelings, sensations and experiences, without evaluation, interpretation or attachment. But it is this last component, the process of identification with the content of consciousness—and the sense of self that arises as a consequence—that is the most difficult thing for us to see, so it is to further consideration of notions of selfhood that we now turn.

SELF KNOWLEDGE

Human beings know an awful lot of stuff. Far more than any one person could ever possibly hope to comprehend. But there's probably even more that we don't know and almost certainly a good deal we simply can't know. And I don't just mean things we don't know yet but one day will. I mean stuff that we can't know, ever. Stuff that is simply unknowable. And perhaps the ultimate unknowable concerns the very fact of existence itself, or why anything exists in the first place. How, for example, do we explain the emergence of conscious life from inert, lifeless, matter? We can't. We don't even know whether we're asking the right question, never mind how it is possible for us to ask that question in the first place. Confronted by the brute fact of our fundamental ignorance, we are forced back on ourselves. But that's okay, because everything we really need to know has—if we but knew it—already been revealed to us, which is why ancient wisdom is as relevant today as it has ever been. So, we accept what is, as it is. We take a step back from the frenetic activity with which we distract ourselves to avoid facing the truth, and we simply abide in the deepest reality of what we are, the fundamental intuition of being itself. I am and I know that I am.

Surprisingly, this turns out to be the greatest enigma of all.

Meditation is often talked about as a means of cultivating self-knowledge. Contemplation of the unfathomable mystery of consciousness, which we experience as the deepest reality of what we are, is, ultimately, the point of meditation. But what is the deepest reality of what we are and how do we come to know it? We undoubtedly have the experience of being a conscious subject—a self—but is this something we've learned, or is it innate? Is it something that's really real, or merely a fictional construct? And what is consciousness anyway? We are certain that it exists, but we have absolutely no idea what it is. The self is at once both the most familiar and the most mysterious fact of human experience. Just as the eye cannot see itself, except in a reflection, so the self cannot know itself, except as reflected in other people. It is in others that we see our common humanity; it is therefore in others that we may learn something about ourselves reflected back to us in their behaviour. We come to know ourselves by seeing ourselves as others see us, and others as we see ourselves.

Oddly—sometimes unnervingly—the path of self-enquiry may reveal that the self as we normally think of it, the self of our ordinary everyday experience, is a construct; a story projected by multiple layers of attachment to, or identification with, the various phenomena that are mistakenly assumed to be I, me, and mine. This is neither a 'good' thing nor a 'bad' thing. It is simply a natural process by which a sense of identity is constructed. It becomes a problem, however—and life gets bumpy—when we take the constructed self to be real in ways that it simply isn't. For it is the constructed self that experiences, and as often causes, the suffering and unsatisfactoriness that is the hallmark of the human condition. Meditation is, therefore, about learning first to see, and then to let go of, those myriad attachments from which we construct our sense of self, in order that we may be free from the bondage of our conditioning.

Individual personality is accorded high status in our contemporary self-understanding. It may not always have been so, but it is undoubtedly now the case that the individual, and its supposedly inherent rights—most particularly the right to freedom of choice—is of paramount value and importance. Moreover, our personality is uncritically assumed to be unique. It is, we instinctively feel, somehow who and what we really are. This is rather ironic when we consider that the word 'persona' derives from the word for the masks worn by actors in classical Roman drama to distinguish the different characters in a play. Far from being something fixed or essential, our personality can more appropriately be thought of as a mask, a performance of ourselves that we present to the world. Who we are is essentially a work of fiction. This fiction serves a useful purpose at one level, but is ultimately not what it appears to be, and can often be the cause of no end of trouble when taken to be more real than it really is.

And yet, it is clearly the case that as we go through life we ordinarily experience ourselves as a thinking, feeling, autonomous subject. We experience being an 'I' who is the experiencer of experience. This 'I', or sense of self, is the subject of our thoughts, feelings, memories and fantasies; it is the thinker, the feeler, the owner of those thoughts, feelings, memories and fantasies. We assume that this 'I' has some sort of stable and fixed identity that endures through all the changes of life. We suppose that this experience of being a subject, the sense of personal identity we undoubtedly have, constitutes our true self. After all, our own subjectivity is surely the one thing of which we can be certain when all else has been stripped away. And yet...

Because we imagine and feel that we are that subjective

experience, and that it is our true self, we also suppose that it is what is most real about us, that it is who and what we ultimately are. And, moreover, since we are able to experience our subjectivity even when not conscious, such as in a dream—and thus dissociated from our physical senses—we might suppose that it must also have some sort of autonomous existence independent of the body. The self is thus envisaged as being somewhat analogous to the driver of a car, or software on a computer. Indeed, our speculations about the self may go further still. If we can conceive of the self as having a reality that is separate from the body, then it is but a small step to the notion that the self does not really need a body at all, but exists by virtue of its own essential being, and may even be immortal and eternal. This is the common notion of the soul, believed to be the truest reality of who and what we are. The trouble is, however, that although the sense of self feels instinctively right and true, is completely normal and—arguably—necessary, as soon as we start to think about it in more detail, and try to put our finger on exactly what this sense of self really is, we find that it eludes our grasp. Although we intuitively 'know' there is a self—or, at least, we have the unmistakeable experience of being a self—whenever we try to locate that self it disappears like a puff of smoke.

Just try and imagine who or what you *really* are. There is nothing we can say or think that will come anywhere near to giving us the full story. For example, we cannot reduce the totality of who and what we really are to our bodily form alone. If we were to suffer an unfortunate accident and lose a limb, we would not think that we were not still fully the person we have always been. Nor can who and what we really are be reduced solely to our mental experience either. Which mental experience would we choose? Are we our memories? Our hopes and fears, desires or regrets? Which ones, in particular? Nor can I fully describe myself in terms of my occupation, qualifications or experience. Anything I might say about myself could be completely true, but it still wouldn't be a complete account. It wouldn't be anything like the whole truth, because it would say nothing about who I am in relation to family members and friends. These descriptions also would be true, but not the full story because they reveal nothing about my beliefs, opinions, political convictions, likes and dislikes. And so on, and so on. Any sentence that begins with the words "I am..." may be true at one level, but at another level will also be false. To give an account of personal identity that claims to be ultimately real and true, a complete and definitive statement, is to pass off fiction as fact. The only true thing I can say about myself is that I am not, really, fully, truly any of the things I can say that I am. All the characteristics with which we identify are part of who we are, or have become—and all may be true—but none are the whole truth, none can be said to be 'it'. And the self cannot simply be equated with consciousness either, because the sense of self persists when we are unconscious. Taken together, what does it all amount to? When I try and imagine me, my self-image is a blurry composite of people I have been, depending on which memories come to mind. I may imagine myself at an ideal, indeterminate age, or I may have some romanticised image of myself in the role of someone I would like to be. The truth of the matter is, of course, that none of these images is real: we are none of the thoughts we think we are. The self is a fantasy. A story we narrate about ourselves.

When we look at the various phenomena we suppose to be our 'self', what we actually see is a constant flow of experience. Nothing more, nothing less. It's simply consciousness being conscious. Ultimately, perhaps, it is just conscious of itself. What keeps the wheel turning is the naturally arising tendency for 'our' consciousness to evaluate, and thereby identify with, the various phenomena of experience—because it is in the nature of consciousness to be conscious *of* something—and to take those experiences, those sensations, thoughts, memories and so on, to be a self, to be 'my' self. We act, for sure. But there is no actor. There is just acting. As we go through life, doing the things we do, we quite naturally assume that there is someone who is the doer. But when we look for that someone, no one can be found. Most of what we do is done without any conscious act of will whatsoever. We just act automatically, reciting well-worn scripts, performing our familiar roles, playing out patterns of conditioned behaviour, learnt over time and reinforced by habit. That sense of self, which we undoubtedly do have, is nevertheless just a notion, a constructed identity, projected onto the events of our lives, and creating the illusion of continuity, meaning and purpose.

We are so caught up in the illusion of personal identity, imagining the construct of self to be real in a way that it simply isn't, that we fail to see things as they are. What we call the self is but the semblance of something we imagine to be an enduring entity, a 'something', separate from our bodies, which we think is who and what we *really* are. Upon closer analysis, however, in reality this sense of self has no essential being. It just a notion we have, the result of a process of false identification with various constantly changing and naturally occurring phenomena, which arise and cease without any such 'self' being involved. What we call a self is in fact an outcome of attachment to—or identification with—all that is *not* self. This is completely normal, neither right nor wrong, but the point is what we imagine to be the self it is essentially a story we tell about ourselves, rather than actually being the self itself. And because the sense of self is taken to be more real than it really is, so we experience all the suffering and unsatisfactoriness of life that characterises the human condition.

ATTACHMENT

I f what we call the 'self' is to be defined as a collection of attachments, then the question is what, exactly, do we mean by this word 'attachment'? Simply stated, our attachments comprise all the various phenomena of experience with which we identify as I, me, or mine. The notion of 'I' is the illusion of being the 'owner' of 'our' experience, which in and of itself consists of a series of impersonal phenomena that arise and cease in a beginningless, endless process of constantly becoming something else. The process of attachment is the unconscious habit of identifying with the phenomena of experience, with the 'stuff' of life, which then gives rise to all the stories we tell ourselves in which the central character appears to be an independent, self-existing, autonomous 'self' that I imagine to be 'me'. Understanding attachment is the key to understanding ourselves, and the prerequisite for attaining freedom from attachment. As we will know from other areas of life, the first step towards changing a habit is becoming aware of it. Becoming aware of attachment is the purpose of meditation.

We commonly talk about being attached to things, and usually mean by this some sort of sentimental attachment to material objects, such as our prized possessions, special gifts or family heirlooms. This feeling of attachment is such that if we were to lose that thing, it would make us sad. But the attachment is not really about the thing, or any qualities it may have, so much as the way our sense of identity is bound up with whatever it may be. The reason the loss of it would make us sad is because we define ourselves in terms of that thing; we see that thing, whatever it may be, as being in some way an intrinsic part of who and what we are. To lose it would be to feel that we have lost part of ourselves. Attachment is not primarily about the object of attachment, but our relationship to it and, specifically, how we invest our identity in it – whatever 'it' may be. Thus, the notion of attachment extends far beyond the ordinary sense of attachment we may have regarding some of our worldly possessions. Attachments are the fundamental building blocks from which our sense of self is constructed.

Understood this way, our attachments are *whatever* we identify with and however we define ourselves. This obviously includes material possessions, as well as our physical bodies and the things we enjoy experiencing. But our attachments are not limited to the clothes we wear, the things we own, the brands we like and the activities we enjoy. We also create attachments in relation to many other 'things' that we think we 'own', such as our memories and opinions, our thoughts, feelings, hopes, fears, ambitions and achievements. Attachment is our sense of who we are in *all* aspects of being, including the social conventions and ideological commitments we live by, and our notions about what should or shouldn't be the case in any given circumstance. Attachment, in other words, is everything that we take to be I, me and mine. It is everything in which our sense of self is invested, everything with which we identify, everything we think we own and, most of all, it is the sense of being the owner that arises from all of that attachment as a result. Attachment is the fuel that enables the fires—of greed, hatred and delusion—to keep burning. It is the fuel that sustains our suffering, that feeds the creation of the personal identity illusion, the mistaken notion of the one who suffers. Attachment is the process by which we define ourselves into being. It is not part of our identity; it *is* our identity. And, like the layers of an onion, it goes all the way down.

We live in a world of nebulous half-truths, imagining it to be made up of static, stable entities. This helps us get by. It is necessary that we see things this way. But it is an illusion. Reality cannot be pinned down: it is dynamic, complex and multidimensional. Our minds try to simplify our experience of the totality of what is by trying to contain it and reduce it to sentences. But no sentence can ever capture the fullness of reality as it is in itself. Even the simplest of circumstances defies a complete explanation. But still we grasp at the various fleeting phenomena of experience, clinging to illusions of solidity, ignoring the fact that all such phenomena are ephemeral and ultimately insubstantial. This is not 'bad' or 'wrong'. In fact, it's completely natural. Attachments serve a useful purpose in normal everyday life. If we did not have a sense of personal identity we would not be able to function or even survive. Instincts of self-preservation would not be possible without the notion of a self in need of preserving.

However, problems arise when we are too attached to our attachments, when we think they really are who and what we really are, when we fail to see that attachments are just attach-ments, and not the self as such. This is true of everything with which we identify, but it can be especially so with regard to the tendency we sometimes have to attach to negative identities, or when we get into the habit of playing a part that then becomes expected of us. Of course, we all play various parts we've picked up as we've gone through life. It's a crucial part of growing up, as we struggle to work out who we are by awkwardly playing whatever role is deemed fashionable at the time, like trying on different outfits, none of which quite fit. Tragically, this can sometimes include adopting self-destructive identities, in order just to be seen to be someone. It can take years to break free of our conditioning – and many of us never even start on that journey.

Our attachments are our baggage. And we go through life burdened down by an enormous amount of excess baggage, some of the most burdensome being our attachment to our opinions about what we think should or shouldn't be the case. We are conditioned by our baggage, the accumulation of attachments and the stories to which they give rise, which we imagine to be our personality, but which is really only a series of masks we present to the world. We can see our attachements playing out every time we unthinkingly react to a situation, or enact one of the various scripted behaviours we have unconsciously rehearsed over the course of our lives, like a playlist of familiar tunes. Our attachments are presented as the various addictions, compulsions, irrational fears, superstitions, delusions, naïve hopes, assumptions, prejudices, expectations, habits of speech and action that we identify as 'me', and project onto the world. As a result, our journey is often heavy going, laboured and difficult. We blunder our way through life, with our projected self made up of all those bulky attachments, clumsily bumping into things—mostly other projected selves—getting hurt and hurting others along the way. Many of the problems we experience in life, whether we are aware of them or not, are a consequence of our baggage, our attachments or, more specifically, the habit of mistaking our attachments for this notion of a self: being too attached, in other words, to our personality, our mask. Wouldn't it be so much easier if we could travel light?

Attachments become the stories we make up about how we think things are, as we go through life superimposing onto the reality of 'what is' a version of what we think should or shouldn't be the case. Our attachments are the lenses that cause us to see things the way we want to see them, rather than as they are themselves – even in the face of evidence to the contrary. And it's going on all the time, mostly without our even being aware of it. We just don't notice, as over the course of a lifetime, we lay down patterns of behaviour, habits, and conditioning until they become so ingrained that we think the story we have been telling ourselves is what is actually real and true.

Through meditation we may come to see that we are not our stories and, at the same time, that a story is all we are. We learn to see the mind as if we are a detached observer, seeing that thoughts are just thoughts, that the little judgements we make about each and every moment of consciousness are arbitrary and not ultimately real and true. We learn to see how the process of attachment and identity formation unfolds, and that what we call I, me, and mine is a game played within our thoughts. We learn to see how the game works and how even the detached observer who sees this can so easily slip into becoming yet another attachment. But the good news is that to see it is also to see how to stop it, by not allowing those thoughts to become I, me, or mine, by not trying to hold onto things but just going with the flow that is what is instead. Now we see that the flux of phenomenal experience is how things are—there are no static entities, no reified self—all is the flow, the flow is all. And the sense of self, too, is just the mind in time. So rather than trying to identify with bits of experience and say 'that's me', we just become one with the flow, which is not this or that but just is what is. We are not our thoughts, and—at the same time—the flux of transient experience, that is what is, as it is, is all there is, and therefore is all we are.

Meditation is about learning to see our attachments for what they are—the hindrances that block our path, the baggage that bumps into life, the projections that come between us and reality as it is—so that we can be free of the ways in which those projections determine our behaviour. This is why meditation is so often described as learning to see things as they are. Not merely as an intellectual exercise, but because the false notion of self is the root of all our existential suffering, and the ultimate cause of the frustration and unsatisfactoriness that characterises the human condition. The truth of existence is that all things pass away. They cease to exist. We create the idea of permanence in order to shield ourselves from this fact, but that only makes things worse. The idea that we are a 'self' arises as a result of a natural process of habitual identification with the transient phenomena of experience. As such, it cannot but result in suffering, as we are inexorably parted from the attachments out of which our identity is constructed.

As we have seen, the notion of attachment extends far beyond our material possessions to include our thoughts, feelings, memories and desires – everything, in short, with which we identify as I, me, or mine. More importantly, attachment denotes not just what we think we possess, but the notion of the one who purports to be the 'owner' of those possessions in the first place. Possessions give rise to the idea of the one who possesses. To put it another way we are, quite literally, possessed by our possessions. Not only in the way that they influence the circumstances and manner of our lives, but more profoundly, in the sense that they actually create the construct that we take to be the self in the first place. Attachments are thoughts with which we are so closely identified that they become who and what we think we are. We might describe them as obsessive thoughts, so intense that they literally possess us. Who and what we think we are is, therefore, nothing less than a form of possession.

DETACHMENT

Deep down, we instinctively know that something is not quite right in the world. We know, from our own everyday lived experience, that life presents us with innumerable challenges. There is much that is not as we would like it to be, though most of the time we fail to see where the problem really lies. The fact is, we cannot hope to resolve anything until and unless we learn to see things more clearly, most especially our own nature. This is why meditation is described in terms of the cultivation of self-awareness. That doesn't mean it's all about indulging in a deeper and more intimate experience of ourselves, but rather that it's about cultivating an awareness that, paradoxically, transcends the limitations of individual selfhood. Meditation helps us see things as they are and break free of our conditioning by learning that we are not our thoughts, that they need not control us, and that the way we feel about the world may not reflect the way the world actually is. What we are, if anything, is not so much the thoughts and the stories of which we are the subject, but the awareness that lies behind those thoughts. When we talk about meditation as the cultivation of awareness, we are not talking about striving to become more keenly aware of things in the world—we're not talking about being aware of anything in particular—but rather abiding in the simple experience of awareness itself.

Meditation is an exercise in taking our attention away from our thoughts, in order to connect with the deeper reality behind them, the fundamental intuition of being we all share. The cultivation of awareness necessarily entails, therefore, the cultivation of compassion, for the notion of self-awareness is meaningless if it does not imply awareness of the self in relation to others. By acquiring a greater understanding of how our own mind works, we gain a degree of insight into how all minds work. Self-knowledge is emphatically not a solipsistic endeavour: it entails knowing others. True self knowledge is to know ourselves as others, and others as ourselves. This is why we talk about meditation as taking a step back—from our sense of self, ultimately—in order to put things into perspective, which is to say, in order to see things in relation to a reality beyond or other than the self. In the simple but endlessly profound practise of quietly observing the mind we gain that perspective by cultivating a certain degree of cool detachment. We observe the mind as if watching a movie, rather than being in it as the star of the show.

Detachment, however, is a word that can carry negative connotations, so it is important that we are clear about what we mean by it. Sometimes, for example, people equate the notion of spiritual detachment with an attitude of lofty disengagement from the mundane business of everyday life. Surely, it will be argued, it is important to do the things that need doing, to strive for change where change is needed, to oppose injustice, to resist oppression, to take the initiative, to put things right. If we are simply detached, we will not engage with all the stuff that needs sorting out. It is solipsistic, complacent and in some cases irresponsible, they will say. And there is an element of truth in this point of view, in as much as spirituality can tend towards being introspective and self-indulgent. But being detached is not the same thing as being disengaged, so we must be careful not to confuse them. Of course there are times when we need to address matters that require our attention. Detachment is not about avoiding responsibility, or not confronting issues that need to be confronted. On the contrary, it is precisely by being a little detached—from our sense of personal ownership, ultimately—that we are able to be *more* engaged.

It's also important to realise that being detached is not the same as being aloof or remote from others, as is sometimes suggested. The cultivation of detachment within the context of meditation is not about being detached from others but from oneself, or to be more precise, from our attachments and all that we think we possess but which in reality possesses us. It is about detaching from our egocentric sense of self. Far from making one aloof, a little healthy detachment makes us more, not less, connected with others. In other words, the ability to detach from self-interest makes us more compassionate, more empathetic, because we are more able to be truly present to others if the obstacle of our own self is out of the way. Detachment is being able to put things into perspective. It is being able to see things clearly, as they are, in themselves, rather than only from our own personal point of view. The practise of meditation is the practise of detachment, learning to detach from the sense of identification with all the things we take to be I, me, and mine. But far from being a recipe for solipsistic complacency, or passive inertia, this is actually what enables us to be more involved, and more able to act effectively, to sort things out, address issues and do what needs to be done.

If I had to choose one word to sum up the essence of the spiritual life, a strong contender would be 'selflessness'. All spiritual teachings commend altruism, condemn egotism and very often promote some degree of self-denial. Arguably, virtues such as love and compassion, which are often seen as being of supreme value, are based on a prior foundation of selflessness. Those who would follow the spiritual path are called to forsake themselves and give up all that they have, and—we might add—all that they are, or think they are. But it's difficult, is it not, to be selfless – even at the best of times? Not least because a degree of self-interest is an important and healthy survival mechanism. And that's okay. The problem comes when the ego takes over, when we lose ourselves in self-absorption and cannot tell the difference between who we are and the baggage we have become.

Seeing things for what they are is the first step towards freedom from our conditioning, from the prison of the ego, and therefore from being the one who suffers. Meditation, the cultivation of awareness, the practise of detachment, is the means by which we come to see that we are not our thoughts, we are not our attachments. Through it we learn how to unpack our baggage, rather than identifying with it; how to put it to one side, rather than letting it take over our lives completely.

PART III

WHY MEDITATE

A PROBLEM TO SOLVE

When people ask me how to meditate, the first thing I want to know is why they want to do it in the first place. Our motivations determine not only what we do, but also how we go about it and, above all, what we will get out of it. When it comes to meditation, the exact same practice can lead to very different outcomes, depending on the intention behind it. Some people take up meditation because they have heard it might help them with anxiety and stress. Others may have come to it within the context of a faith tradition. And the commercially driven need to market ever more novel applications of mindfulness has seen it promoted as the means to achieve everything from a competitive edge in business to a more fulfilling love life. This is not about deciding between 'right' or 'wrong' reasons for practising meditation. The point is that if meditation is about the cultivation of awareness, then being aware of why we want to meditate in the first place might be a good place to start.

My own interest in meditation was initially awakened by reading books about Buddhism. It was only some years later that I came to the realisation that reading books alone wasn't enough. I had to learn how to do it. When I eventually got around to attending classes, it soon became apparent that I really hadn't a clue what I was doing, but I did at least have a sense of why I wanted to do it, however naïve or misguided it might have been. Over time, my reasons for persevering with the practice subtly started to change, as indeed the practice itself subtly started to change me. Presumably, you too have at least some degree of interest in meditation—otherwise you wouldn't still be reading this book—and this presumably also implies that you have some reason or other for wanting to take that interest further. Even if you've been meditating for so long that it's just something you do and you don't really think about it anymore, or if you reckon you already know the answers to those questions, we will always learn something new if we keep asking. Our motivations very often change over time and our reasons for wanting to start meditating might be quite different from our reasons for wanting to continue. And sometimes, our motivations are not what we think they are.

Why are we interested in meditation? What difference does it make to us? What is the issue that we think meditation might resolve? It doesn't matter too much what the answers are. The more important thing is being aware of the questions. People have all sorts of reasons for wanting to meditate, from the reduction of stress or improvement of performance to deepening their relationship with God or seeking enlightenment. These days, and certainly in western societies, meditation seems most commonly to be promoted as a tool to enhance wellbeing, in some way or other. Given the number of health conditions in which stress and anxiety are often thought to be a factor—from depression to heart disease—this is surely a good thing. Meditation is also increasingly being marketed as a technique to improve mental performance, creativity, decision-making and productivity in the workplace, and we might want to see these as positive developments as well.

However, there is a certain irony about the use of spiritual exercises that were originally designed to dissolve the ego being used to reinforce it. Meditation reduced to 'nothing but' a technique for self-improvement or an aid to personal well-being is fine, as far as it goes, but if that's all it is I can't help thinking we might be missing out on something. It is, of course, a good thing to cultivate wellbeing. Taking care of ourselves, paying attention to our mental health, having a positive experience of life rather than being miserable – these are all important. But personal wellbeing focussed, as it inevitably must be, on the self, is not the primary purpose of meditation, even if it is a welcome side-effect. To see meditation simply as a tool to enhance wellbeing seems rather limited when it can take us so much further. The spiritual endeavour has traditionally been about transcending the ego, going beyond the self, not feeding it. If we lift our eyes to scan more distant horizons we may come to see meditation as the antidote—rather than an accessory—to the contemporary secular religion of consumerism.

INTENTIONS

There is so much more to meditation than it just being something to help us cope better with stress, feel good about ourselves or boost our productivity. If we practise in order to reduce the symptoms of stress, we may well succeed. But that will be it. Reducing meditation to this merely functional level, without giving adequate consideration to the intention behind the practice, fails to recognise the fact that everything we do has a moral implication, one way or another. So how are we to evaluate our motivations? One approach could be to try and discern the question to which we believe meditation might be the answer. This is something we each have to determine for ourselves. Is it merely a matter of wishing to address a particular problem in our life, or are we seeking some sort of deeper transformation of the whole of life itself?

When we consider the narratives around mindfulness and meditation that currently seem most prominent in the media and in public discourse, we hear a lot about stress and well-being on the one hand, and performance and productivity on the other. These are really two sides of the same coin: meditation as a tool to help us achieve more. This, in turn, relates to our pathological need to affirm and expand the ego, to have greater 'impact' or to feel better about ourselves. Meditation can be practised in pursuit of a variety of goals. But not everything we do that requires our undivided attention is necessarily a pathway to enlightenment. It is the intention that counts. There is something rather incongruous about the notion of using a meditation app on our smartphone in order to help us cope better with the intensity of life in the digital age, not to mention mindful eating to aid weight loss or mindful dating to help us find the perfect partner. These popular trends reveal and feed our neurotic obsessions with physical appearance and the egocentric need for affirmation. Rather than enabling us to break free from our attachments, using mindfulness and meditation in these ways is more likely to reinforce them.

If we examine our reasons for being interested in meditation, and our motivations for wanting to practise it, we will very often find that at least part of the story has to do with some issue or other to which we believe meditation could provide a solution. Often—though not always—people come to meditation in order to resolve a problem and feel better. There could be a specific issue that we need to rectify, or some area of life we would like to improve. It could be something to do with stress or anxiety, or it could be about recovery from addiction. It could be a response to a personal crisis, or part of a commitment to a spiritual discipline. All these, and more, are among the reasons people may decide they want to take up meditation.

There is, however, a problem inherent in the problem-based approach to meditation, which is that very often all we are doing is treating the symptom without addressing the cause. If we feel we need to meditate in order to cope better with stress, it implies that we have cultivated a stressful life-style. We get stressed, so we do some meditation to make us feel better in order to be able to carry on doing everything that causes us to get stressed until we need to meditate again! If we meditate merely in order to be able to function better under adverse conditions, without doing anything to change those conditions, then we are really only adding to the problem by building up a tolerance, rather than actually solving it. Would it not make more sense to deal with the cause of the problem, so as not to have it to begin with? Instead of developing coping strategies in order to feel better, why not make everything better so that we don't have those problems in the first place?

This tendency to focus on the symptoms rather than the causes is very evident in the promotion of meditation as a means to achieve specific outcomes, rather than as a holistic approach to the transformation the whole of life. I have heard people say that they followed a recommendation to practise some calming meditation exercises in order to help them cope with a particularly stressful phase they were going through. But as soon as their situation improved, they stopped doing the exercises. The person concerned may be in no doubt that the exercises were beneficial. But it doesn't occur to them that a regular meditation practice might be beneficial in more ways than just dealing with one specific issue, that it might be beneficial to life in general, not least in preventing problems from arising in the first place. Meditation is not just about fixing problems, but changing our perspective so that we can see and address the underlying issues. It is true that meditation calms the mind. This is one of its most obvious and immediate benefits and often the reason that people are attracted to meditation in the first place. But that's only part of it, and if we stop there, we are potentially missing out on a great deal more. The point is it calms the mind and that in turn enables us to see things more clearly, including some of the deeper aspects of the issue we might be wanting to address through meditation.

Sometimes our 'problems' are a matter of perspective, and may simply vanish as a result of seeing things differently. After all, the sky is always blue, whether or not there are clouds obscuring our view. And sometimes our problems might be more intractable. Either way, our everyday experience clearly indicates that life comes with all sorts of problems, and indeed some are so fundamental that we even talk about the problem of the human condition.

THE PROBLEM

If it is true that we meditate because we believe it will be the solution to some sort of problem, it is undoubtedly also true that we often misidentify the real nature of the problem. The real problem is not necessarily the problem as it presents itself to us. The problem of stress, for example, is not that we are stressed, but that there is something about the way we live our life that is causing us to experience stress. The solution is not to learn relaxation techniques in order to ameliorate the effects of stress, but to remove the causes of stress by making significant changes in our lives as a whole. The problem, therefore, is not some particular detail of life—not the presenting issue, whatever it may be—but the underlying factors that condition every aspect of our experience of life in the first place.

One thing that many traditional religious narratives provide—and which is often lacking in discourses of secular spirituality—is a sobering assessment of the experience of being human: a realistic account of why life is the way it is, or why things are, in short, somewhat less than ideal. In Buddhism, for example, the observation that the whole of human experience is stained by an all-pervasive and deeply frustrating sense of unsatisfactoriness is encapsulated in the notion of *duhkha*. Usually translated as 'suffering', *duhkha* refers to much more than simply physical pain or emotional hurt. *Duhkha* is the frustration of not getting what we want and having to put up with what we don't want. The fact that life is fraught with physical suffering should be obvious enough, but the Buddha also insisted that even the pleasures of life imply *duhkha* because they will inevitably pass away, leaving sadness, regret or some other form of pain, however subtle it might be. *Duhkha* is therefore based on another notion: that everything is impermanent. When I saw this for the first time it struck me like the proverbial thunderbolt. Of course, nothing lasts. Absolutely nothing. Impermanence applies not only to our bodies and mental experiences, but also ideologies, rules and regulations, social institutions, cultural conventions and the whole universe. In the final analysis, *duhkha* results from the identification—or, more accurately, the misidentification—of our selves with things and experiences that are contingent and impermanent. This includes our material possessions, our constantly changing physical body, our memories, achievements, status, values, preferences, weaknesses, hopes and fears. Everything, in short, with which we identify as I, me, or mine.

This is not to say that life itself is inherently flawed, but

rather that human beings make it so – a fact surely confirmed
by our own experience. Existence, in and of itself, is a pure
and marvellous thing, and is what it is. The suffering and
unsatisfactoriness we experience as a fact of *our* existence
often—though, of course, not always—has a lot to do with *us*.
Not getting what we want. Having to accept what we don't
want. Suffering, in this sense, is the consequence of all the
myriad forms of attachment that give rise to the notion of the
experiencing—and suffering—subject. But it is not only within
Buddhism that the human predicament is seen like this. In the
western tradition, the Biblical story of the Fall of Adam and
Eve functions in much the same way as a foundational narrative to explain the problem of being human—the fact that we
find ourselves in a less than ideal state of profound alienation
—which in Christian terminology is referred to as 'original
sin'. We tend to associate sin with rules and regulations—and
a morbid sense of guilt—but the words translated as sin, in
both Hebrew and Greek, suggest the idea of 'missing the
mark'. The notion of sin denotes our failure to see things the
way they are. It is a sort of primal ignorance, and it is the
suffering that inevitably follows. The notion of the Fall, like
the concept of *Duhkha*, provides an account of the experience
of being human. As a result of the Fall, human beings find
themselves alienated from God—or that which is real and true
—and condemned to experience life as pain, conflict and
struggle. As such, it is the story that has shaped the world in
which we live, for human beings are mythological creatures,
constructing narratives of meaning from the stories we tell to
explain why things are—or are experienced as being—the way
they are, and what we might be able to do about it. Perhaps
most tellingly of all, in both the Christian and the Buddhist
accounts, the principal cause of the suffering and unsatisfactoriness that characterise the experience of being human is
our misplaced desire.

Coming to some sort of realisation about the problem of the human predicament, together with a strong urge to do something about it, are the two factors that constitute almost any kind of spiritual awakening and the consequent search for deeper meaning and fulfilment that people use the language of spirituality to describe. Sometimes it takes an existential crisis to provoke this awakening, which then leads to the practise of meditation. Sometimes the practise of meditation, undertaken for some other reason, will lead to a spiritual awakening, which may then alter our intention towards the practice. One day, we suddenly see through it all. We realise the emptiness and unreality of everything, and we embark upon the only journey that was ever worth making: the quest to discover who and what we really are. Once we realise that the world 'out there' is mediated through, and often actually constructed by, the self, we realise that to know the self is to know everything we can possibly know. And yet it is the hardest thing to do, for the self we know and experience is the self we have to unravel and deconstruct.

Meditation is simply the practise of quietly observing the mind. By doing this we start to notice things we might normally miss; we get to know ourselves a bit better, learning what makes us tick and what presses our buttons. By seeing how our own minds work, and learning about our own behaviour, we learn something about the fundamental, universal nature of human beings in general, and the worlds we create and share with others. With this knowledge, we improve our ability to make better decisions, manage difficult feelings and generally live life more skilfully. Watching the mind, and observing the thoughts as they come and go— anxious one minute, happy the next—we are able to see that thoughts are just thoughts. And, most importantly of all, that we are not our thoughts; or, to put it another way, that 'we' are just our thoughts! Sometimes, for example, we may have a thought or experience that makes us anxious. So we tell ourselves not to worry about it. But, of course, that just makes it worse: we can't stop thinking about it. We become identified with it. But because we are not our thoughts, or because our constructed self is nothing but our thoughts, the simple discipline of taking our attention away from our thoughts takes away the power of those thoughts. In the act of seeing our thoughts objectively—rather than subjectively—we automatically cease to identify with them. By seeing them as just thoughts, rather than *my* thoughts, we deconstruct the sense of self that has become attached to those thoughts, that thinks it is those thoughts. Simply by gently returning our attention to the breath, again and again, we can, with practise, learn to direct our mind away from negative or unhelpful states – and also to cultivate positive ones. Instead of identifying with our feelings all the time, without even realising that's what we're doing, we grow better able to see them for what they are. By not identifying as the 'owner' of our experiences, we do not let those experiences own us.

We can only address our 'problems' successfully if we can see them for what they really are. If we learn to see things more clearly, what we will very often discover is that the heart of the problem, the biggest problem we have, the problem behind all our problems, is the problem of being the one who has the problem. In other words, our greatest—and, ultimately, only problem—is the sense of self that attaches to, or identifies with, the various states of being that we experience as problems. Until and unless we tackle that fundamental issue, we will never really solve the things we experience as 'our problems', for they are just symptoms of the underlying malaise of the self. By learning to see the way our minds work, we learn to see the way life works.

PEACE AND POWER

There are two basic human motivations, applicable both to meditation and pretty much everything else we do for that matter, which can be epitomised as the desire for peace and the desire for power. We yearn for peace with regard to the regrets of the past, which we cannot change; and we crave power over our anxieties about the future, which we cannot control. And lying behind both of these impulses, of course, is fear. Life as normally—that is, unskilfully—lived, is driven by the attempt to do anything we possibly can to avoid facing our fear.

The reasons people give for wanting to meditate vary widely, but they very often tend to fall into one of two general categories that can be summarised in terms of relaxation, on the one hand, and self-improvement on the other. Together these form a spectrum that has the attainment of peace at one end and the acquisition of power at the other. Indeed, it is interesting to note how frequently the words 'peace' and 'power' appear in the titles of books on spirituality. Narratives of peace and/or power permeate the ways in which meditation is taught, described, and written about. You may be able to notice it in the way people talk about meditation, disclosing either their desire to find inner peace in order to counterbalance the stress in their lives, or a thinly disguised quest for some kind of power, such as may be revealed in the desire for improved performance or higher knowledge.

When understood in terms of the attainment of peace, meditation tends to be associated with the kind of approach that promotes it as an antidote to the pressures of modern life. Meditation will undoubtedly help in this respect. Almost anyone who tries it will find they feel more relaxed and calmer as a result. It certainly works as a tool to relieve stress and anxiety. But to practise meditation solely in order to gain peace of mind seems to fall short of the radical transformation, of oneself and the world, advocated by most spiritual traditions. There are plenty of ways to relax, if that's what we need to do, such as by going for a walk, engaging in a favourite hobby or just having a nap. A meditation practice focussed exclusively on our own personal wellbeing risks becoming deeply self-indulgent. Peace of mind is important, and not to be dismissed as a triviality, but true peace involves a great deal more than just learning a couple of techniques to relieve the symptoms of stress. True peace is a sense of profound harmony between the self and the world, the deep integration that is, paradoxically, the consequence of a certain kind of detachment from 'the world'. And that takes some doing.

At the other end of the spectrum we find those who want to meditate for the sake of self-improvement. This could include anything from enhancing our powers of concentration so as to do better in business or sport, to the quest to find God or achieve enlightenment. Like the desire for peace, there seems, at first glance, little to object to in a desire for self-improvement. But it depends what lies behind it. To meditate in order to improve one's competitive edge in business may be motivated by desires that come from, and serve to reinforce, the selfish ego. Even the quest for enlightenment may be tarnished by a personal desire for esoteric knowledge or experience – and the power that we may imagine comes with it. Any approach to meditation that sees it in terms of self-improvement—however 'spiritual' that self-improvement may appear to be—ultimately serves to feed our vanity and become another ego-trip. As the great spiritual teachings often make clear, the desire for enlightenment is ultimately an obstacle to enlightenment.

Peace and power characterise not only the range of our personal motivations but can also be seen in wider social trends. We strive to acquire peace and power in our lives; and we see this striving writ large in the societies in which we live. Advertising exploits these motifs relentlessly, selling us illusions of comfort, confidence and control, in order to make us spend money we don't have on things we don't need under the false impression that possessing whatever it is will make us happy and complete. But consumerism is an insidious lie. It is not about satisfying our desires by getting what we want, but the perpetual stimulation of desire so that we constantly want something else. And what we want is not really the the thing itself, but the person we imagine we will become as a result of acquiring it. We increasingly demand, and expect, instant gratification, because that gratification is essentially the affirmation of the self. Whatever we want we must have—because it is our right, because we deserve it—and we aren't prepared to wait. But this does not make us happy; it makes us into slaves. And behind this obsessive compulsion to have and to own—and thereby construct our identity—is our old friend fear.

Fear sells. Fear drives the need we feel to consume, the need to fill the emptiness we secretly know is there but can't admit, the need to want whatever it is that we imagine will make us feel complete, will make us feel safe and lay all our fears to rest. After all, our basic instinct is to survive, to perpetuate our existence, both in this life, and in terms of whatever may or may not lie beyond it. Consumerism is a warped expression of the survival instinct corrupted by a false promise of fulfilment, a delusional escape into fantasy that avoids the truth of impermanence and the reality of our inevitable mortality. It is no accident that people will gobble up anything that promises youth, health and longevity – however far-fetched and implausible the sales pitch. We are no less irrational and superstitious than our pre-industrial forebears. We will believe—and buy—anything that promises to shield us from the terrors of ageing, sickness and death. But it will never work. We mistakenly imagine that fulfilling the desires for peace and power will liberate us from the prison of our fundamental anxieties: namely, regret for the past we cannot change and fear of the future we cannot control. It won't. Freedom is undoubtedly the ultimate goal, but it will never be reached through the pursuit of peace and power.

The twin desires of peace and power, which one way or another, and in various different guises, represent our funda-mental motivations for pretty much everything we do, are not in themselves necessarily right or wrong. They can be positive or negative, and they permeate both life in general and the spiritual life in particular. The point is learning to see how they are at work in ourselves and in the world around us, to see where the sense of self is in all of it, because peace and power are simply the egocentric expressions of the balance and perspective, the calmness and clarity, which meditation helps us to develop. Behind the pursuit of peace and power lies the desire for freedom—essentially the same desire for freedom that lies behind nearly all our motivations—only in a form that will lead not to freedom but deeper attachment.

Meditation as the cultivation of calmness and clarity, by contrast, leads to the the dissolution of attachment.

Meditation is the solution, not just to the presenting issue of this or that anxiety, stress or 'problem', but the fundamental problem of human existence itself—of birth, ageing, sickness and death—because it exposes the root problem of our habitual identification with the notion of being the one who experiences the problem to begin with. It is the solution to the problem of the human condition because it teaches us not to fear fear, enabling us to accept who and what we are, as we are, and reality as it really is. Through the practise of meditation we learn to overcome fear by coming to see that the real problem is the notion of the one who is afraid. Ultimately meditation is not about finding peace or acquiring power. It is not about de-stressing, alleviating the symptoms of some problem or other, or even seeking enlightenment. Rather, it is about understanding the true nature of the self that either wants or rejects these things in the first place.

The problem is not peace or power in themselves, of course, so much as where the motivation to acquire them comes from and the need it seeks to satisfy. Different people clearly use meditation in pursuit of different goals, and there will be a range of views regarding the merit or validity of these various aims. As motivations for meditation, however, both peace and power are likely to reinforce our tendency to think in terms of objectives to be attained, and thus the illusion that we are the beneficiary or 'owner' of the fruits of our endeavours. If you meditate in order to achieve peace and power you may well be 'successful', but you may also miss something much more important. Meditation is not really about anything that can be achieved, or a result to be gained. The object of meditation is to be in a state of meditation. It is its own end. Peace and/or power, in one form or another, may indeed accrue to the practitioner of meditation, but whilst these are among the consequences of meditation, they are not the purpose of it. Not that there is anything wrong, at one level, with wanting to improve one's mental and emotional quality of life; the point is that focussing too closely on the detail may cause us to lose sight of the whole. Whether one is motivated by peace or power, therefore, the issue is much the same: such motivations basically serve to reinforce the ego, whereas the purpose of meditation is to transcend the sense of self altogether.

DISCIPLINE

One of the traps people often fall into, when faced with all the choice available in the meditation marketplace, is to keep flitting from one teaching to another, thinking that if only they can find the best method, then all their problems will be solved. Unfortunately, this is a delusion: it just doesn't work like that. There is no perfect practice. Whilst it is entirely reasonable to shop around a bit to begin with, and sample a few different techniques, once you find something that suits you, that seems to work, that fits, then the best thing you can do is to stick at it. But this is often easier said than done. One of the most difficult things about meditation is sustaining a regular personal practice. However much we may know it is good for us, the truth of the matter is that—if we are honest with ourselves—much of the time we do not really feel like doing it. Much of the time it can be diffi-cult, and often it is simply boring. And we will always be able to think of something more important or appealing that we feel we should be doing instead.

The cultivation of awareness entails radical personal trans-formation—a whole new way of seeing things—and that is not usually something that just happens overnight. What is more, it may even be something that we try to resist, whether consciously or not. We will find that it is hard to change the habits of a lifetime, just as we often find it hard to learn a new skill. It can be difficult to muster the discipline and motivation we need in order to engage in a regular meditation practice, especially when we take into account the demanding work commitments and family responsibilities that are such a significant part of everyday life for so many people. And yet, the discipline and motivation necessary for meditation are really no different to the discipline and motivation needed to go on a diet, give up smoking, take more exercise, or pursue a new hobby – all things that most people are able to manage if and when they really want to.

Meditation is a spiritual discipline that, like physical exercise, is something we have to do regularly in order to maintain and improve our condition. Like physical exercise, meditation involves a process that a part of us may be unwilling to undergo. Like physical exercise, we can easily be put off. Committing to a regular meditation practice is not a soft option. It invariably involves struggle and may bring us face to face with some uncomfortable truths. Unlike physical exercise, however, we cannot set targets or track the 'results' of meditation. There are no measurable outcomes that we can evaluate; we cannot really quantify progress in any way at all. But we can usually feel a difference, even after just one session, and even when we think our meditation has not gone particularly well. Sometimes we have to take it on trust that it is worthwhile, which is why thinking about our motivations is so important. When we feel it is pointless, or that we are not making any 'progress', having a good reason to maintain the discipline can be vitally important. And, in spite of it feeling like a waste of time, we may actually find that by sticking at it we reap benefits we are not even aware of until we look back and see how much things have changed over a period of time.

Although discipline is, for many people, a word that conjures up negative connotations of punishment and repression, we should remember that it is also a word that has meanings to do with instruction and learning, which we use to refer to a skill, training or field of expertise. Like any other kind of discipline, commitment to a meditation practice has a simple rationality. Anyone who has studied for an examination, gone on a diet, or trained in order to get fit, is already familiar with the basic principle: some form of sacrifice in the present for the sake of a reward in the future. I know full well that I should eat less and exercise more and, admittedly, it is quite difficult at times to make myself do it. Any excuse will be sufficient to put me off. But it is possible. It can be done. The discipline required for meditation is no different.

Like anything worthwhile, cultivating a meditation practice takes effort: a certain amount of strictness is necessary, rather like pruning a plant in order to stimulate its growth. Having said that, our regime should not be excessive. If we force ourselves to undertake a degree of discipline that is too severe, or engage in exercises that are too strenuous, it can impair our health and make it impossible to maintain any kind of practice at all. Extremes of discipline can be harmful in other ways too. Making a show of how spiritual we are suggests pride rather than holiness. Feeding our vanity with the supposed approval of others might make us feel good about ourselves, but that is all it will do. It will not bring about genuine transformation. In fact, it will probably impede our spiritual growth. Therefore, a properly balanced discipline should be understood as a middle way that is neither repressive nor indulgent. The purpose of discipline, in the spiritual life, is not to punish the body but to purify the mind.

Discipline is largely an individual matter, but it also has a corporate dimension. Sometimes we need to remember that we are not isolated, autonomous individuals. Human beings are social animals. We exist in relation to others, as members of groups and communities. And in any kind of group or community, it is some form of discipline that enables people who may otherwise have little in common to work together or live alongside one another in relative harmony. Discipline is about taking responsibility for who and how we are in the world, whilst the lack of it is a critical factor in much of the social disintegration we see all around us. In this context, discipline is not restrictive but rather the essential mechanism that actually allows the life of a community to flourish.

Corporate discipline and personal discipline sustain and enable each other. For example, many people will appreciate the advantages of meditating in a group. Being part of a group imposes a shared discipline that supports and encourages us in our own practice, as we hold the silence for each other. But we also need a degree of personal discipline in order to function as a group in the first place, whereby each member endorses the tacit agreement to abide by a certain discipline for the sake of everyone else. Meditation is a personal practice, but it is not private: it has an impact beyond the self. If it doesn't affect the way we behave towards the other people with whom we share our world—and also, therefore, the world itself—then what's the point of it?

PERSEVERANCE AND PRIORITIES

Sustaining a meditation practice requires a certain amount of effort and discipline. We have to want to do it. And we have to stick at it. In order to do that, we presumably have to have a good reason, whether we are fully aware of it or not. Because it is hard, sometimes, to keep going. It is hard to make time, every day, especially when it may seem as if we are not getting any 'better' at it. It is hard to stick at it, especially when it seems boring or pointless, or when we are busy with other things. And it's easy to tell ourselves we are no good at it or it's not making any difference. Often, of course, this is just when we need meditation the most. Meditate an hour a day, goes the well-known and probably apocryphal quip attributed to a number of people – except when you're busy. Then make it two. Yet, despite knowing how important it is, our meditation practice is very often the first thing to slip. We need constantly to remind ourselves that it is a priority. To anybody who says they don't have time, I would point out that we always manage to make time for the things we really want to do. The thought that we don't have time to meditate is just that. A thought. We can observe it and let it go, together with all the other thoughts about all the important things we need to do. Are they as important as our need to meditate? This is not to say things don't need our attention—of course they do —but do they need it *right now*? It is a question of priorities, which is why understanding—or at least being aware of—our motivations is so important. If we don't see meditation as a priority in our lives it will be difficult to cultivate or maintain the habit. Indeed, like so many things, once the initial flush of enthusiasm has faded, we may just stop trying altogether.

And yet, straightforward as it may seem—in principle, at least—there is something rather incongruous in all of this. How is it that meditation can seem like such hard work if, as we're so often told, it is simply a matter of realising our true nature, of just being who and what we already are? Whilst it is certainly true that to meditate is to abide in the deepest reality of what we are, the fact is we have accumulated a life-time of delusion-reinforcing habits and consequently we have lost sight of what lies hidden beneath all the layers of our constructed self. It takes time to undo all that. Time that can seem unproductive if we are looking for instant results. But just as we would not expect to understand all there is to know about quantum physics after a single lecture, or to lose weight after a single workout, so we should not expect to achieve 'enlightenment' after a single meditation session. We all know that we can never hope to achieve anything in life unless we stick at it, whether this is learning a new skill, going on a diet, or getting fit. We have to commit to the discipline. Meditation is the same. We start again every time we sit. In fact, we start again every time our mind wanders.

The need for perseverance should be obvious enough, yet we are fickle creatures, on the whole, with a tendency to blame external circumstances when, more often than not, the problem is as likely to be our own unwillingness to take responsibility for ourselves. I constantly allow myself to be put off by the slightest inconvenience, or to get side-tracked by what might appear to be more attractive options. Most of us will no doubt be familiar with the experience of thinking that the grass is greener on the other side of the fence, even though we know it never is. Yet how often do we allow ourselves to be seduced by some fantasy about how our lives will be complete, if only some detail or other could be changed in such and such a way in order to make things just the way we want them to be.

Given our expectations of instant gratification—as if it is a basic human right—it is no wonder that many people seem to think that perseverance, remaining stable and rooted, implies a rigid stubbornness that is repressive and can only lead to stagnation. But perseverance has nothing to do with stagnation, or stifling creativity. Rather, it is to stand firm and be persistent. Perseverance is precisely what enables us to rise to the challenges presented by life's inevitable changes. It implies engaging fully with the situation at hand, and remaining committed to a course of action, in spite of obstacles or distractions. This should not be taken to imply a fatalistic attitude of just passively accepting everything life throws at us without demur. Sometimes there are things that ought to be challenged. But it requires careful discernment, and an understanding of the fact that challenges can also be an opportunity for growth, that engaging more effectively sometimes requires us to take a step back and put things in perspective. Constantly flitting from one thing to another, by contrast, or failing to take responsibility by blaming others, will be more likely to increase our frustration than resolve it. Perseverance is, ultimately, what will enable us to overcome the conditioning of our constructed selves in order to become who and what we really are.

In spite of the times when life—or just our meditation practice, for that matter—seems bleak or even hopeless, it is perseverance, rather than giving up when we cannot be bothered to make the effort, that gets us through. Perseverance enables us to create those positive habits that help sustain us on the journey. Unfortunately, however, we are often unwilling to do more than the minimum required to achieve immediate results, not realising that as a result of even just a little discipline we will almost certainly gain more than we will lose. But it takes a degree of trust to make a commitment for the sake of an outcome that cannot be known in advance. However, we should be able to see something of the truth of this in our own everyday experience. Mastering a skill, establishing a career, or even just getting to know somebody, are ordinary examples of things that cannot and do not just happen instantly, but take time—perhaps even a whole lifetime—and only come to fruition as the result of sustained commitment.

As with any discipline, meditation requires time and effort. If we manage to stick at it, however, we may be able to cultivate sufficient mindfulness to maintain our focus and avoid being led astray – at least for a few moments. Thoughts will not cease as long as there is breath in the body, but their constant flow might slow down a little. If and when this happens, we may experience a gap opening up between them. This inner space is truly silent, truly empty. In its stillness it is timeless, because time implies movement. Abiding in this gap, free from all the noise and clutter with which we normally fill our minds, we may experience an awareness of the still centre behind the surface activity of our conscious mind. We may find that we have stopped repeating our mantra. We may even stop breathing for a few seconds, without realising it, forgetting for a moment our physical discomfort, or indeed that we are a body at all. We may have the feeling that we are unlimited consciousness, pure essence of being. In this still, silent, empty space that is simply what is, we may become aware of the simple, basic, experience of reality as it is in itself, the fundamental intuition of being that is the deepest reality of what we are.

Although, of course, as soon as we realise it, we have had another thought – and it's gone...

WHAT REALLY MATTERS

The experience of being human can be characterised as a perpetual search for satisfaction, whether of our physical desires or personal goals. This implies that at some level we must instinctively feel incomplete. After all, we would not need to seek satisfaction if we already had it. If we continue to examine our pursuit of satisfaction, we may come to see that chasing after all the things we think we want does not bring us lasting contentment, but only further frustration and resentment. The pursuit of pleasure for its own sake does not bring satisfaction but disappointment, just as drinking to get drunk does not bring happiness but misery. Yet still we are driven—in everything we do—by some sort of instinctive urge to strive for whatever it is we imagine will result in our complete and perfect fulfilment, will make me fully the 'me' I really want to be.

This seemingly innate yearning for 'something more' rests on the assumption that things—the world, life in general, myself—are, or are experienced as being, somewhat less than ideal. We live in an imperfect world of illusion and appearances, which is deeply riven by pain and suffering. In addition to the obvious manifestations of physical suffering—such as violence, sickness and poverty—there is also what we might call existential suffering, which we experience as the frustration of not getting what we want, the compulsion to pursue desires that are out of reach or cannot be fulfilled, and the disappointment of never gaining true satisfaction. In short, all this 'unsatisfactoriness' comes about because we do not see things the way they really are, we are not in tune with reality as it actually is. Our illusions about the way we think things should or shouldn't be clash with the way things actually are, giving rise to what we might call the problem, whether real or imagined, of being human; the problem to which we believe meditation might be the solution.

If we want to understand our motivations we should ask ourselves a very simple question: what do we really, really want, finally? In other words, what *really* matters? We will need to keep asking this question over and over again if we want to get to the bottom of our desires and motivations. Generally speaking, we don't really know what we really want, so a conflict arises within us between our needs and our desires, which inevitably overflows into our lives. If we want to resolve this dilemma, we will need to understand the difference between what we really want and what we think we want, which is also to understand why we are really doing what we are doing, and what we really hope to achieve by it. We have to be able to see what is being fed when we act out the scripts of our constructed selves, and how the sense of self is reinforced by the stories we tell and the roles we play, whether intentionally or not. And we need to discover what it is that will instead bring us true peace and contentment, completely and finally. What is the satisfaction we seek in order to relieve ourselves of the restless agitation of our never satisfied desires, once and for all? What, in other words, *really* matters?

Try to explore this question, and see where that exploration takes you. What do you end up with? There may be many things you desire, many different conditions you may wish to be in, but which, if any of them, will bring you lasting fulfilment? Will whatever it is you think you want really bring permanent happiness, peace and satisfaction – completely, absolutely, finally? If we explore this question, we eventually end up with... with what exactly? We cannot say. In the end, we may simply reach a wordless horizon, beyond all the enjoyments we already know and the satisfactions we can imagine. It is just 'what really matters'.

And we have to keep at it. At times the process may be heavy going, uncomfortable, disturbing even. We may have to undergo a complete re-evaluation of everything we have previously taken for granted. The practise of meditation, undertaken with diligence, will inevitably challenge our most fundamental assumptions, and undermine our fragile sense of security in the 'things of the world'. In a very real sense, then, embarking upon this journey is likely to bring not peace but discord, at least to begin with. The struggle that is entailed in the serious engagement with a meditation discipline soon puts paid to the popular notion many people seem to have that it's all a lot of self-indulgent 'navel-gazing' to make us feel better about ourselves. The truth is, there is nothing easy about it. Approached with the seriousness it truly demands it may be one of the most challenging enterprises we are ever likely to undertake, for it requires nothing less than that we give up our precious notions of who and what we think we are, in order to become who and what we really are. Far from being a crutch, or a coping strategy, following this path forces us to throw away our crutches, and lose much that we may previously have thought important, including—or perhaps, especially—our precious sense of self.

This image of struggle and conflict presents a sharp

contrast with much contemporary popular spirituality, where the emphasis often seems to be on self-help, personal affirmation, and the fulfilment of our emotional needs and desires, implying in turn that it is only meant for people with problems. This is not to say that the spiritual life is not about wholeness and healing—of course it is—but the wholeness in question is not so much about comforting the self but dismantling it altogether in order to heal the breach that separates us from the reality of the way things are. The 'problem' we are here to solve is not our lack of personal or emotional fulfilment but the underlying cause of our existential suffering, namely the profound alienation and all-pervasive unsatisfactoriness that characterises the human condition as expressed so succinctly in concepts such as *duhkha* and original sin.

To follow this path is to turn away from the unskilful living that is the consequence of not seeing things the way they are and turn instead towards that which is ultimately real and true. This means giving up self-centredness and re-orienting our lives in relation to a reality that is fundamentally other than self. The resolution of personal problems may well be part of that, but it is not the sole point of it. The point is waking up, which also, as it happens, resolves everything else as well. If the only purpose of our practice is to focus on our personal issues we are likely to miss out on the greatest benefit of all. There is so much more to meditation than self-care and wellbeing. Indeed, it has the potential to turn our lives completely upside down. But in doing so it also offers us the possibility of gaining true and lasting freedom.

THE SEARCH FOR MEANING

Modern life is busy, full of stress and anxiety. We've all got far too much to do and, generally speaking, it seems we're not very happy about it. If we are to believe what people say about themselves, then being too busy would appear to be the number one affliction facing people in contemporary western societies, although sometimes we parade our busyness as a virtue, perversely even making it a source of pride. And yet, at the same time, our busyness very often acts as a thinly disguised mask to cover our profound but unacknowledged boredom. This is deeply ironic, but what else could explain our chronic addiction to superficial entertainment and mindless distraction? How is it that we are so easily taken in by the escapist narratives of advertising and the empty gloss of celebrity culture? Why else would fantasy seem so much more attractive than reality if we didn't have the spirit of boredom gnawing away at the innards of our soul?

Our insatiable craving for distraction—and our propensity to give into it—can be seen as a symptom of the illusion that our minds are separate from our bodies. Since the mind is never present, whereas the body can only be present, we exist in a state of perpetual alienation from our own reality. And so we crave the distraction of constant stimulation to fill the void created by this fundamental lack of integration. Even though we know that being over-stimulated by constant distraction doesn't make us happy or fulfilled, but rather leaves us feeling anxious, frustrated and depleted, still we fall for it. And even though we also know, just from ordinary experience, that we feel most alive when we are fully engaged with reality as it is here and now, when mind and body are in one and the same place, still we remain glued to the very screens that purport to connect us to the world but actually separate us from reality, and reinforce that profound alienation.

The feeling of vitality that comes with the experience of being more fully integrated is sadly much rarer than it could and should be. Most people, most of the time, live in a state of dis-integration, which we generally just call 'stress'. There are lots of ways in which we can experience stress, but what is typically meant when people talk about 'being stressed' is the feeling of not having enough time to do all the things we think we need to do. Stress is very often not actually caused by the thing we're doing, but rather the plague of distracting thoughts about all the other things we think we should be doing instead. Giving our full attention to one thing can be immensely satisfying, whereas trying to do something whilst at the same time worrying about lots of other things dissipates our energy and may even stretch us to breaking point. Of course, there are numerous external causes of stress, and these will need addressing on their own terms. But it's also true that the experiences we label as 'stress' are frequently associated with the absence of body-mind integration.

This fundamental lack of integration could also explain why we seem to live in a world in which everyone is apparently searching for 'something more', something that will satisfy our deepest yearnings in a way that is somehow never quite accomplished by the fulfilment of merely superficial desires. The implication seems to be that searching for 'something more' is a constant feature of the human condition – and that may well be so. I'm sure it is true for many people, although it would appear not to be a primary concern for everyone all the time. That said, even if it would be going too far to suggest that everyone is consciously searching for spiritual fulfilment, it is plainly true that everyone is seeking fulfilment of some sort, one way or another – be that in the form of wealth, success, happiness or pleasure. The instinctive feeling that there must be 'something more' to life than this, however that may be imagined, is by definition a 'spiritual' concern—whether expressed in those terms or not—for it is ultimately to do with the meaning and value of our existence.

The fact that we feel this fundamental lack, and imagine there must be something more—and are capable of abstract reflection on it—is a consequence of our capacity for self-awareness. It is a commonly held assumption that this is a uniquely human attribute. Other animals, by contrast, we believe, do not have any sense of why they do what they do. They just do it. They do not have the capacity to reflect on why they are alive, and what may or may not happen after they die. Humans alone, it seems, have the ability to project a meaning and a purpose onto their lives, both individually and collectively. This may or may not actually be true, and our existence may or may not *really* have meaning and purpose, but it is undoubtedly the case that we believe it to be so, and arguably it is necessary that we have this belief, not least to maintain the illusion of our sanity. But we may just be kidding ourselves. We may not be all that different from other animals after all. We may just think there is a meaning and purpose to our lives—and indeed from our point of view, it might seem that there is—but is there really? Does humanity really have a *purpose* as such? Does the universe really care whether human beings exist or not? We'll never know. And indeed, it seems quite absurd even to ask the question.

Perhaps it would be safer to assume that there is no intrinsic meaning to being human other than the meaning individuals make for themselves. To believe that the truth is 'out there' seems like wishful thinking, a delusion closely related to the delusion of our uniqueness, which is arguably responsible for all the suffering that we both experience and cause. We may be utterly convinced that it *should* be so, but that doesn't mean it is. It would seem we need to create meaning—even where there isn't any—and this may actually be part of the problem rather than the solution because those narratives of meaning always imply a disjuncture between reality as it is, and our beliefs about how we think it *should* be. Why can't we just *be*? This, more than anything, should make it clear that meditation is not about goals. It is not about what we can achieve or gain for ourselves, which makes the popular emphasis on meditation as a tool to boost productivity and improve performance seem all the more ironic. In spite of what some may think, meditation is not something we do for what we will get out of it, but an end in itself. The purpose of meditation is to be in a meditative state. That's it.

People generally take up meditation because they are attracted by some perceived benefit they believe it will provide; a notion that it will help to resolve a particular issue in life. Some might be attracted by the hope of spiritual enlightenment. Many more, these days, seem to see it as a therapeutic intervention to relieve the symptoms of stress or a self-help technique to enhance our capabilities. And there are multiple variations on these two basic themes, epitomised—as we have already seen—in the ego-driven desires for peace and for power. But I would like to suggest a different way of looking at it. Meditation is not so much about what it will do for us but what it might do *to* us. If meditation is the practice of learning to be more present to reality as it is, then it is about cultivating a more balanced approach to life, putting things into perspective and seeing things as they really are, rather than as we think they should or shouldn't be. Seeing things more clearly, seeing what is really going on in our minds and in our behaviour—and being aware of our conditioning—gives us a genuinely meaningful choice: to act with intention, rather than just blindly reacting to circumstances beyond our control. Meditation is about learning to see our personal baggage and the attachments that control us. We cannot address something if we are not aware of it. Seeing this is the first and most important step on the path to freedom.

FREEDOM

One of our most powerful motivations in life is the yearning to be free, which we experience in all sorts of different ways. But what actually is this freedom that we all want? And does this talk of freedom imply that we are not free? Isn't this counter-intuitive? Surely the notion that we are essentially free agents is a fundamental characteristic of being human? Surely the suggestion that we are not, in fact, free is a claim that most people would instinctively reject? I would argue that in spite of these commonly held assumptions, we are nevertheless profoundly constrained, slaves to our conditioning and circumstances and, therefore, not free at all. We are thoroughly programmed, brainwashed even—by culture and by habit—and consequently governed and controlled by forces of which we are not always fully aware and over which we are certainly not the master. Indeed, much of the time we are not even really living life, but going through the motions, living in fantasy worlds, whether of our own making or, more likely, fed to us by the media we consume.

To make matters worse, we now live at one further remove from reality: not only in our heads but through a screen. We walk down the street, our attention glued to the screen in our hands, headphones plugging our ears, oblivious to our surroundings, not even looking where we're going. We're sitting with a group of friends, all playing with our smartphones rather than actually talking to each other. Whether at home, at work, or out enjoying ourselves, almost everything we see or do, including our interactions with other people, is meditated through a screen. We go through life with a screen constantly in front of our faces, showing us reality represented as entertainment, a fantasy that we're fooled into believing is real. But it's not. The algorithms are just becoming better at showing us the world as we want to see it. And with every click we feed this insatiable monster, enabling it to spread like a cancer that saps our vitality and imprisons us in a bubble where all we see and hear is, ultimately, just a commodified reflection of ourselves.

There are so many ways in which we are not free. Technology is supposedly meant to make our lives easier, to free us to be able to... to do what exactly? To be manipulated by advertisers? To consume mindless entertainment? To get wasted? To play games? We cannot handle freedom. We do not even know what it really is. We think it's about freedom of choice, freedom to do or not to do the things we do and don't like, the freedom to gratify our desires. It's not. That kind of freedom, wrongly understood, is in fact a deeper and more binding form of slavery. And we are all slaves. To make matters worse, even if we're aware that we are not as free as we would like to be, our most common assumption about freedom—that it is synonymous with freedom of choice—actually reinforces our lack of it. In the consumer society, choice is the trademark of the fully realised individual. But choice, and the further implication that this is how we gain control over our circumstances, is in fact the ultimate illusion. The truth is our choices are all made for us, long before we ever get to 'choose' anything. Far from being a recipe for happiness, so-called freedom of choice feeds the illusion of being in control that actually takes away real control, rendering us powerless and unable to make our own decisions. Ironically, the more choice we have, the more helpless and inadequate we feel. Keeping our options open leads not to freedom but frustration, indecision, and fear of missing out on more attractive alternatives. And so we meekly collude with the myth that life would be so much better if only we could live the dream planted within us by the media. This is not freedom, but yet another form of slavery. True freedom is not the freedom to indulge our every whim, but freedom from our pre-programmed and self-centred desires for gratification; freedom—ultimately—from attachment, that is, identification with the various constructs of who and what we think we are.

The belief that freedom is equivalent to freedom of choice presupposes an autonomous subject or agent of free choice. And indeed, it is commonly assumed that the human individual is a rational agent, able to act freely. But it may not be so. Though it is deeply counter-intuitive, there are arguments to suggest that free will and the notion of the autonomous subject may, in fact, be an illusion. This is neither the time nor the place to enter into these debates in any detail, except to say that whether or not we *really* have free will, it is clear that in spite of the instinctive feeling that we are free agents, the truth is much of our behaviour is conditioned, whether by the culture in which we live, our own life experience, or the all-consuming power of consumerism. If we could just see things a little more clearly—see the scripts that determine the parts we perform—then we might be a little less controlled by our programming. Even if we can't wake up from the dream, we might at least become aware that we are dreaming. This is the awakening that is so often alluded to when talking about the goal of meditation. It's not that there is an alternative reality, beyond the world we know, into which we awaken, but rather it's about becoming more self-aware within the only reality there is: namely, this one. But if we cannot even see the problem—our conditioning and attachments—we have no chance of being able to do anything about it.

To make one final point, it is important to realise that our freedom is not ours alone. Personal freedom comes with corporate responsibilities. This is something that people very often forget, especially those who would define freedom in terms of personal choice or the absence of externally imposed restrictions. We live in a culture in which the autonomous right of the individual to seek his or her own fulfilment has become the highest good: being true to oneself is all that matters. But what does it mean to be true to oneself if that 'truth' does not also include a sense of responsibility for the welfare—and freedom—of others? If the deepest reality of what we are is the ground of being we all share—the fundamental awareness of being itself—then at a very profound level we are all connected, and therefore accountable to, and responsible for, each other.

AWARENESS

Meditation is all about the cultivation of self-awareness, but this doesn't necessarily mean that it causes us to become self-absorbed. Yet many people clearly seem to think that meditation is self-indulgent, an impression not helped by the emphasis in some forms of contemporary spirituality on self-improvement and personal fulfilment. To be fair, there may be some approaches to meditation that could be said to support that view. There are trends within the contemporary secular mindfulness movement, for example, in which the emphasis is very clearly on meditation as a means of manifesting our personal, and often explicitly materialistic, desires. Such tendencies are a far cry from the teachings of people like the Buddha or Jesus, not to mention countless others besides them. There is a huge difference between being self-aware and being self-absorbed; between self-improvement and self-transformation. It may be true in one sense that the self is the only reality we know, and that in the end we are all alone. But it is also the case that the opposite is true: we are what we are by virtue of our relationships with others. No attempt to cultivate self-awareness can ignore the reality of the common humanity—the fundamental essence of being—that we all share, together with the need to take responsibility for the impact of our actions on others.

Meditation is the practice of taking the focus of our attention away from ourselves, away from our own thoughts, away from the constructs of self that our thoughts make manifest, away from our illusions and attachments – even if only for a few moments. In doing so, we learn to be more present, to ourselves, to reality and to one another. We get a glimpse of freedom: freedom from the ego. And when we do this, when we strip away the ego stuff, we find that we're all pretty much the same behind the mask. This, in turn, enables us to connect with the deepest reality of what we are, the reality that is what is. We realise that all that we think we are is at some level an illusion, a construct; it is not really what is completely true about us. We are, of course, unique individuals—each with our own store of experiences that have formed us—but at the same time we also share a common human nature. This is true not only in terms of our physical biology, but in terms of our psychology too. In spite of all our many varied and wonderful differences, human beings basically operate in more or less the same way. Similar hopes and fears drive me as drive you; similar things hurt us, similar things heal us. And that's because the process of attachment, the construction of the sense of self, is universal – regardless of the myriad different forms it can take. Meditation is not about being deeply absorbed in our own little world. It is profoundly relational, for it opens us up to a new, less egocentric, way of seeing things: as they are in themselves, rather than as *we* think they should or shouldn't be. This is true liberation, because it is liberation from the solitary confinement of the ego. And, in turn, seeing that at some deeper level

we share a common reality, and that we share the same suffer-
ings, releases compassion into the world. This is how meditation makes us better people, and the world a better place.

Therefore, when we talk about meditation as an exercise in
the cultivation of awareness, we are not talking about
spending time having an intimate experience of ourselves, but
gaining a deeper understanding of the true nature of the self.
And that could turn out to be something rather different to
what we expected. Awareness gives us the capacity to see
ourselves and what we do objectively. Any degree of genuine
self-awareness is inextricably linked to awareness of that
which is other than self, for true knowledge of the self only
comes from seeing it as the object of another's awareness. To
know the self is to see ourselves as others see us, and to see
others as we see ourselves, and to know that at some deeper
level the distinction is an illusion: I and thou are one and the
same. To know the self is to know the clay from which all pots
are made. It is to know the deepest reality of what we are, the
ground of being we all share. It is to identify with consciousness itself, rather than any particular manifestation of it; with
the essential rather than the incidental.

CALMNESS, CLARITY AND COMPASSION

The purpose of meditation is not merely to reduce stress or
enhance performance but to learn how to be free of our conditioning and attachments. Meditation thus has three transfor-
mational learning outcomes: seeing things as they really are,
living life more skilfully and growing in awareness and
compassion. Learning to see things more clearly, as they are
rather than as we think they should or shouldn't be, depends,
in turn, on cultivating calmness of mind. Calmness of mind
results in freedom from stress and anxiety, and this is what

allows us to see things more clearly. As a consequence of that clarity, we may learn to live life more skilfully, better able to act intentionally rather than always and only reacting blindly. Above all, seeing things more clearly, with balance and perspective, enables us to see our attachments, giving rise to greater self-awareness and the compassion that inevitably flows from a profound realisation of our common humanity. This sense of deep connection leads to freedom from self-centredness and release from the prison of our own ego.

The first and most obvious effect of meditation is, therefore, calmness of mind. Even someone trying meditation for the very first time will probably find that they feel calmer and more relaxed after the session than they did before it started. Feeling somehow calmer is the almost automatic outcome of simply anchoring our attention to a single object of awareness, such as the breath, or a mantra—or both, for that matter—in order to keep it from running after every passing thought and fancy. A deliberate intention to take our attention away from our thoughts and hold the mind steady will naturally cause it to slow down and become more still, because we are essentially giving ourselves a break from all that busyness and, above all, from ourselves. Even if that were the only outcome of meditation it would still be enormously beneficial, not least in alleviating the symptoms of stress and the many health conditions associated with or exacerbated by it. But this is only the beginning. The point of calming the mind is not just to relax, de-stress and be more productive, but to engender clarity of mind. A bucket of muddy water will eventually clear if it is left to be still. Similarly, a still, calm mind will enable us to see more clearly the way things really are, as opposed to how we think they should or shouldn't be. Seeing things clearly, as they are rather than as we are, enables us to put things in perspective and cultivate a healthy sense of balance.

If we are too close to something—either literally or metaphorically—we won't be able to see it properly. The same is true of life. Stepping back is necessary if we want to see the bigger picture. By calming the mind we are able to step back from being caught up in our thoughts, from identifying with the voice in our heads. In effect, we take a step back from ourselves, our stories and attachments and, in so doing, find that we are better able to see and experience things the way they are in themselves.

The clarity of mind that emerges from calming the mind is a result of cultivating tranquillity and equanimity, balance and perspective – or, to put it plainly, sitting quietly and trying not to get caught up in the commentary. The mind will naturally settle down if we keep it present and avoid all the distractions that agitate and delude us, if we don't feed the story by getting involved in it. With that calmness and clarity, we may be able to see that when we are not present it can create a disconnect between us and reality. This disconnect, the difference between the way things are and the way we think they should or shouldn't be, lies at the root of the conflict and tension we experience in life. Through the discipline of being present, quiet and still, observing the content of consciousness, without getting caught up in it, we are able to step out of the running commentary and see it for what it is. We are able to see that our story is just a story, our thoughts are just thoughts. And they come and go without even needing us to think them, because the 'thinker' is just another thought too. We are not our thoughts, and we need not be their prisoner. Seeing things the way they are thus depends upon cultivating a foundation of calmness and equanimity, and a healthy indifference to the thoughts we encounter in meditation. We just calmly let them go without getting embroiled in the story.

However, this is, as has often been noted, easier said than

done. That's why we call meditation a practice. It's something we have to keep doing. Over and over again. But hopefully, with practise, it gets easier. Hopefully, with practise, we learn and grow. That said, sometimes thoughts or feelings may arise that we can't let go, that forcibly grip our attention. In meditation we may learn things about ourselves of which we were previously unaware, just as a result of stopping to look and listen. Seeing things more clearly can have many consequences, which might also sometimes include becoming aware of uncomfortable truths. Knowing what can be ignored and what needs addressing is part of the learning process. It may be a pressing concern, a current preoccupation or a disturbing memory. It may be something that does actually require our attention, even though most of what the mind churns over invariably does not. And the chances are that even something that does need our attention doesn't need it right now. So, let it go.

We have all had the experience of not being able to recall some piece of information, even though we feel that it's on the tip of our tongue. The more we try to think of it, the harder and more frustrating it becomes. So, we leave it. And wait. Sometime later, we suddenly remember whatever it was. Meditation is similar but more intentional. By taking our attention away from our thoughts, away from our storytelling, and thus also taking our attention away from the notion of being the storyteller, we are deliberately learning to ignore our distractions. If we find ourselves wrestling with a knotty problem that we can't resolve, we may find that ignoring it, and being quiet and still instead of worrying at it, will be the thing that enables us to see the solution, which may well have been there all along. Very often we already know the answer; we just can't hear it for all the noise in our heads. The key to seeing things more clearly is learning to ignore our distractions. After all, it is when we are distracted, when we are not really present, that we make mistakes. This is as true in the little things as it is in life in general. If we go through life distracted, or on autopilot, we will have a bumpy ride and make a mess of it. If we are constantly distracted it will have a detrimental impact on everything we do. Taking a step back, putting things into perspective and seeing things the way they really are enables us to act, not just react. Learning to live life more skilfully, by being more present to it, has a positive impact on everything we do, as well as our relationships with other people and also therefore the world around us.

This is how the journey inwards leads us out of ourselves. As a result of the practise of taking our attention away from our thoughts, we become less self-centred. Because we are better able to see things more clearly, from a perspective of stillness and calm, we are more balanced and more reasonable. Because we are more present, we are more compassionate. Because we have cultivated a greater degree of self-awareness, we also have a greater understanding of others. Any genuine inner transformation will also transform our outward behaviour, which inevitably includes our behaviour towards others. Seeing the common experience of being human that we all share automatically releases our compassion. This, in turn, can have an impact way beyond the immediate contact we have with the people around us, as it may also have a knock-on effect on the way those people behave and act towards others too. By learning to see things more clearly and live life more skilfully, we reduce our own suffering, and also the suffering we directly or indirectly cause others. Being more fully present to the reality of other people, rather than existing only within the bubble of our own story, causes us to be more authentic and considerate. All of which, taken together, ultimately contributes to making the world a better place.

And if it doesn't, then what's the point of it?

Our meditation practice can never just be about ourselves. It is not a form of self-cultivation that benefits only the individual meditator. Meditation may be personal but it is not private. If we change ourselves we will change the world too, because we will change the way we relate to it, and therefore also the way it relates to us. A meditation practice always implies, therefore, an ethical context. If the fruit of one's practice is not apparent in one's behaviour towards others, then what good is it? If meditation does not awaken within us a profound sense of humility, compassion and respect for others; if it does not make us better people, and the world a better place, then it is worthless. Meditation changes our behaviour and the world around us because by being more present, more mindful of the reality of others, we act less self-centredly, and this inevitably has a positive impact on the other people with whom we come into contact.

To live life more skilfully is to live life with a heightened sense of awareness, and if there is one thing that meditation is about it is the cultivation of awareness, not just for its own sake but because this is how we develop wisdom and compassion. Awareness is about learning to see—and then to be free of—our attachments, the possessions that possess us. As we have already seen, attachments are all the things with which we identify as I, me, or mine. Not just our material possessions, but our body, our mind and the whole content of consciousness: our thoughts, memories, experiences, opinions, beliefs, hopes, fears, desires and weaknesses. What we are is our attachments. As such, our attachments have a controlling influence on our lives, often in ways that are not at all helpful. After all, it is the projected self, the notion of being the owner of experience, that suffers. It is the projected self that goes around bumping into life, perpetually in conflict with things as they are; it is at best, therefore, profoundly disconnected from reality.

There are many obvious ways in which our lives are conditioned by attachment, whether through identification with personal experience, or the conventions of the culture we happen to inhabit. Social conditioning is all-pervasive, shaping and governing every aspect of our behaviour, often in ways of which we are not even aware. The cultural norms to which we conform, the scripts we act out—without realising that's what we're doing—are reinforced by various means, not least the media we consume. And the most powerful force controlling our lives is consumerism itself: the lie that if only we buy into such and such a brand identity, our life will be perfect and everyone will like us. We are slaves to the dreams of fulfilment sold to us by the media. We are possessed by the possessions that we believe will make us happy. We are in thrall to countless seductive but ultimately empty myths of salvation, whether that be through technological progress, economic fulfilment, or some beguiling fantasy of romantic love and perfect happiness.

Understanding our attachments gives us deeper self-understanding, and also a deeper understanding of others. Not just because we can recognise our own behaviour when it is reflected back to us in the behaviour of others, but because learning to see ourselves more honestly and more clearly is at the same time to see others more clearly too. It is to feel that profound connection with those with whom we share our basic human nature. It is to see things as they are, rather than in terms of our assumptions and prejudices. It is seeing others as they really are rather than as we think they are, or worse, as we think they should or shouldn't be. By practising meditation—that is, simply being still and observing the mind, watching our mental processes in a dispassionate and objective manner and letting go of distracting thoughts—we learn to understand our own behaviour patterns, the scripts by which we operate. Learning to see the workings of attachment, the constructs of self that unconsciously govern our behaviour, we learn to see ourselves as others see us, and we learn to see others as we see ourselves. Ultimately we participate in the pure awareness of consciousness being aware of itself. This is true freedom.

AND FINALLY, SILENCE

Although meditation is generally thought of as a solitary pursuit, there are a number of advantages to practising in a group, and I often hear it said that there is a special energy generated by people meditating together. At one level, this may simply be because of the shared discipline that enables us to create and maintain the silence for each other. The structure of a class makes it easier to commit to the practice, and we are less likely to give up half way through a session if doing so will disturb everyone else in the room. But perhaps even more important is the fact that when we're sitting together with a group of other people—in silence, eyes shut, just observing the mind—all the conventional differences between us, such as race, class, sexuality and gender become quite irrelevant. Everything we think and do, everything that differentiates us from one another, simply disappears in the mutual experience of pure being. Even though we may not know the other people in the room, even though we're just sitting there not saying anything, not interacting with each other, nevertheless we are sharing deeply in the experience of our common humanity. Together in the silence, egos muzzled, we participate in the awareness of awareness itself. Though we are in one sense essentially doing something alone, nobody is left out: we're all in it together. In the stillness of a meditation session we are truly connecting with the other members of the group, united with one another in the deepest reality of what we are.

This is not how people normally interact. 'Normal' social interaction is competitive, a contest for attention. In normal interaction some people dominate, others are excluded. And everyone is performing a role, whether intentionally or not. Silence, by contrast, is a great leveller. In the silence of meditation, everyone is absolutely equal, in a way that turns how we normally see and experience the world completely upside down. Normally we think that we are in all external respects the same, and that inwardly we experience ourselves as unique individuals. But it's the other way around. Externally we are all very different. What we have in common is our subjective experience. The purpose of meditation is to effect some sort of meaningful transformation, not just on an individual and his or her experience of life, but on the whole of life itself. Meditation certainly calms the mind—a benefit that can be appreciated even after just one session—but over time it can also make us less self-centred by enabling us to grow in awareness and compassion. And this is because through meditation we connect with a deeper understanding and appreciation of the common humanity we all share.

Meditation is the practise of stepping back, putting things into perspective, taking our attention away from our thoughts and preoccupations, learning to ignore our distractions, and to see our attachments for what they are. To put it in the simplest terms possible, meditation is about chilling out and getting over ourselves. Calming the mind makes us better able to handle difficult emotions. Seeing things more clearly makes us better able to make good decisions. Learning how the mind works, that thoughts come and go—and that we are not our thoughts—enables us to live life more skilfully. Talking about meditation in terms of calmness, clarity, compassion and connection provides a convenient way of summarising all the many benefits commonly attributed to meditation, including the relief of stress and related conditions, on the one hand, and the cultivation of insight and awareness on the other. The fact that meditation calms the mind also enables us to see things more clearly, not least the constructs of self that obscure realisation of the deepest truth of what we are, the ground of being we all share: the fundamental, irreducible, mystery at the very heart of existence itself.

Thus, we meditate not in order to be good at meditating, nor to enhance the ego by gaining peace or power, but in order to become aware of attachment—the process of identification with the random and impersonal phenomena of experience as if it is I, me or mine—so that we might learn to avoid allowing that sense of identification to take hold in the first place. To be free from the conditioning that results from attachment is to be free from the suffering that characterises the human condition. Seeing things clearly and understanding attachment—or growing in awareness and compassion—frees us, ultimately, from the enslaving habit of identifying with the one who suffers, and causes the suffering of others. Pain is just pain, objectively speaking. But when it is *my* pain, it is suffering. Suffering is personal, subjective. It's about the 'I', the one who suffers. If we can take the 'I' out of the picture—if we can step back from being the star of the movie, or the voice in our head—then we may taste the true freedom of simply being. The pain, or the cause of the pain, might still be there. But it does not only and always necessarily have to be experienced as suffering.

We may or may not be able to change the circumstances of our lives. We may or may not be able to overcome the suffering and damage that we have experienced or caused. But we can change how we see it and how we relate to it. And, most importantly, that means we can change what happens next: we can change how it affects us by freeing ourselves from the controlling influence of our attachments. Meditation is about cultivating awareness, and with it the sense of balance and perspective that comes from learning to take a step back from ourselves in order to see things as they really are, rather than as we think they should or shouldn't be. Meditation brings us into a deeper awareness of, or connection with, the deepest reality of what we are, or that which is ultimately real and true. For some people this may be described and experienced in the terms articulated by a religious tradition; for others it may not. For those who believe in God it is about deepening our connection with God. For those who don't, it's about deepening our understanding of the way things are. In both cases it is about balance and perspective, wholeness and healing and, ultimately, truth and freedom.

That's why we meditate.

EPILOGUE

On Wednesday 19 October 2016, I signed a lease on a commercial property in Newcastle city centre and opened what I will always maintain was the UK's first independent high street meditation centre. Within a year we had a timetable of regular weekly drop-in classes, together with an expanding programme of courses and workshops. At the same time we built up a team of facilitators to lead sessions, and a group of willing helpers to run the Centre. Doing everything on a shoestring budget and relying entirely on the commitment and enthusiasm of a small group of dedicated volunteers certainly presented challenges, but a seed was planted that I believed could have the potential to grow into something really quite remarkable.

Opening the Centre felt like a fitting conclusion to a journey that had begun with that first meditation workshop on the Quayside three years previously. It was a journey marked with a number of key moments, and which drew people to the idea of an approach to meditation that really was *just* meditation. One such milestone was the decision to run a mentoring programme to enable frontline support staff to lead meditation sessions within the recovery projects where they worked. This was a joyful and humbling experience that had a ripple effect almost impossible to quantify. From it emerged a training course for volunteer session facilitators that enabled Just Meditation to develop and grow far beyond the limits of what I was personally able to deliver as the sole meditation instructor.

At about the same time I had the idea of launching a website to try and build an online community of interest in meditation. The first incarnation of Just Meditation was an internet directory of places where people could go to learn or practise meditation, with a database that was searchable by postcode, region, tradition or activities, together with a facility for people to leave reviews and comments. It launched in August 2014 with about 200 entries. But it was hard to maintain, difficult to promote and fraught with technical issues that I didn't have the capacity to resolve. It never really took off, and a year later, I closed it down. In the meantime, the dream I'd long been harbouring of setting up an independent high street meditation centre just wouldn't go away.

Although I can truthfully say that I came up with the idea entirely on my own and before such spaces actually existed, it wasn't long before I discovered that others had clearly been thinking along similar lines. In April 2014, a place called Unplug, claiming to be the world's first secular drop in meditation studio, opened in Los Angeles. The following year a similar venture called MNDFL opened in New York. Since then, secular meditation centres have mushroomed all over the United States. Interestingly, these places all tend to look and feel rather similar—like a Buddhist centre without the Buddhism—and seem to adopt an approach that feels very commercially oriented. They are also clearly aimed at a fairly narrow demographic—young, white, urban and professional— thus confirming all the prevailing stereotypes that label yoga and meditation as middle class hobbies. I knew it would only be a matter of time before something similar appeared in the UK, and sure enough, a little over a year after we opened the Newcastle centre, London's first meditation studio, called Re:Mind—almost an exact carbon-copy of the American model —opened in early 2018.

Critics of the commodification of mindfulness might see these secular meditation studios as shrines to the contemporary spirituality of personal wellbeing, serving to reinforce the narcissistic cult of individualism that traditional spiritual practices were designed to subvert or transcend. Wary of these pitfalls, Just Meditation was developed with quite different goals in mind. I knew from my work with people in recovery that meditation would appeal to a much broader range of people if it could be presented in a less clichéd and more accessible manner. If meditation can potentially benefit anyone, then it should be available to everyone. But all too often it seems as if it is being promoted as something that is really only for those who enjoy a certain kind of lifestyle. The Just Meditation approach maintains that the practise of meditation belongs at the heart of everyday life, and that the benefits of meditation should be extended to a much wider range of people by providing opportunities to learn and practise that are accessible, affordable and available to all.

During the course of 2015, Ollie and I started to talk more seriously about setting up Just Meditation as a charity or social enterprise. We were not clear exactly how things would develop; we just felt we had something worth building on, and that what we were doing could benefit a lot more people. For me, the fullest expression of this vision was always the long-term goal of creating a place wholly dedicated to the learning and practise of meditation, that would be independent and on the high street, though I realised we were in no position to do anything like that yet. Over the coming months we explored various options, refined our plans and eventually incorporated as a community interest company. From then on, things started to move very quickly. We developed a business plan and started applying for grant funding. In spite of thinking that it might take a year or two to grow to the point of being in a position to open a centre, I decided in April 2016 to have a look at a few properties, just to get a sense of what might be available. By early June I had found what we were looking for: the ideal spot to set up the UK's first independent high street meditation centre.

On 22 October 2016 we opened the doors for the first class at the new Centre. Over the next four years the Centre grew steadily, attracting new people and hosting more and more activities, which in addition to the regular weekly drop-in classes, included a wide range of courses and workshops, as well as a seminar series, a book group, a running club and a number of social events. Other groups used the space for their own meditation related activities, and a growing number of practitioners partnered with us to run courses on our programme. In 2019 we formed a new charity to run the Centre, so that it could develop as an entity in its own right. And yet, in spite of the Centre being a great success in all sorts of ways, as a business it was always fragile. We never had enough money and could only barely make ends meet. But by the beginning of 2020 things were looking positive: our accounts showed we were finally on the verge of breaking even, and we were beginning to think about how we could raise sufficient funds to employ a full-time administrator.

Then the global coronavirus pandemic forced the world into lockdown. The Centre never reopened.

GLOSSARY

ATTACHMENT

The sense of identification with objects of experience, including but not limited to material possessions, the physical body, our thoughts, feelings, opinions, memories, achievements, aspirations, regrets, etc. Attachment gives rise to the notion of a 'self' that is assumed to be the 'owner' of the various phenomena of experience.

FEELING

1. A thought or experience with which we are so closely identified (or attached), that we literally become it, and about which we find it very difficult to be objective.

2. The immediate value, positive or negative, attributed to any and every sense impression, usually labelled in terms of attraction, aversion or indifference.

MANTRA

A word or prayer, which may be almost anything from a meaningless sound to a hymn of praise, repeated either as an end in itself or as an aid to concentration.

Examples of two-syllable mantras: So-hum, Thank-you, A-men, Al-lah, Yah-weh, Be-still, Budd-ho, Krish-na, Brah-man, Slow-down, Je-sus, I-am, Let-go, It-is, Clear-mind

MEDITATION

Originally a word for the act of thinking deeply about something; now used as a general term to denote various forms of mental or spiritual exercise, often involving some method of focussing the attention in order to cultivate awareness.

MIND

The stream of consciousness, the processing of mental data, the thinking faculty, the (uniquely) human capacity for abstract reflection and self-awareness.

MINDFULNESS

Can be used to describe both a state of being and also a set of practices designed to cultivate that state. Therefore:

a) An ordinary word for awareness, paying attention and being present; the object of many meditation practices.

b) A popular brand of self-help exercises, including but not limited to meditation.

c) A particular approach to meditation within Buddhism.

PERSONALITY

The constructed self, the mask(s) we project onto the world comprising our attachments.

SELF

1. In ordinary usage our sense of personal identity.

2. In technical usage the constructed notion of personal identity that arises from attachment, the process of identifying as self the transient phenomena of experience.

SELF-AWARENESS/AWARENESS

The purpose of meditation, described as seeing self as other and other as self.

SOUL

1. The notion of a permanent, separate, self-existing and substantial self.

2. The sense of who we really are.

THOUGHT

An assemblage of mental data derived from sense impressions or abstract concepts, and combined into complex mental phenomena (with which 'we' habitually identify as I, me, or mine).

ABOUT THE AUTHOR

Nicholas Buxton is the Director of St Antony's Priory, Durham, creator of Just Meditation and founder of the Newcastle Meditation Centre. He has been practising meditation for over twenty five years, and teaching it for more than fifteen, having studied within both Buddhist and Christian monastic traditions. He has a PhD in Buddhist Philosophy, and is the author of *Tantalus and the Pelican: exploring monastic spirituality today* (2009), and *The Wilderness Within: meditation and modern life* (2014).

ABOUT JUST MEDITATION

Just Meditation represents a distinctive approach to the learning and practice of meditation, through drop-in classes, courses and training.

Just Meditation is independent and inclusive. It neither promotes nor denies any particular tradition or worldview.

Just Meditation is simple and accessible. It is everyday meditation for everyone.

Just Meditation is *just* meditation.

For more information see: https://justmeditation.com

Printed in Great Britain
by Amazon